OTHER BOOKS by MARGARET and ERLING WOLD

Margaret and Erling:

Bible Readings for Couples

Margaret:

The Shalom Woman

Women of Faith and Spirit

GREAT GOD of LOVE

How God
comes to us in our
searching and longing

MARGARET & ERLING WOLD

AUGSBURG Publishing House • Minneapolis

GREAT GOD OF LOVE

Library of Congress Cataloging-in-Publication Data

Wold, Marge.
  Great God of love.

  1. Love (Theology) 2. God—Love. I. Wold, Erling.
II. Title
BV4639.W59   1987   231'.6   87-31915
ISBN 0-8066-2303-9

Manufactured in the U.S.A.   APH 10-2893

1   2   3   4   5   6   7   8   9   0   1   2   3   4   5   6   7   8   9

Dedicated to
Ole and Gunhild, Esther and Frank
the parents
who gave us more love
than we ever sensed or appreciated
and who made real
to us
the love of God

CONTENTS

PREFACE

You want to be loved.

More than anything else, all of us need to be loved.

We've heard that cry in a thousand different ways by many voices and through a variety of actions. The student who struggles for good grades, the athlete who agonizes to make points on the playing field, the woman or man who sobs in our office—all articulate in their own way the need for love.

Ultimately our heart's desire is to know that the One who has created us has not abandoned or forgotten us. Is God pleased with me? Does God accept me? How can I know if I am loved by God or anyone else?

We invite you, in the following pages, to join us on a journey of discovery. We will explore our own hearts and the heart of God to discover a love so elegant and satisfying that it will change and enrich your life.

We long to have you know that you are loved. We want you to see yourself as utterly lovable and worthy. We want to bathe you in the *agape*-love of your Creator who shaped you and fashioned you with the tenderest of caresses and said, when the loving task was complete, "It is very good."

Several years ago we read the words of a Dr. Malone, a psychotherapist from Atlanta, who, after analyzing hundreds of patients, came to a single conclusion: all their needs, though camouflaged in a million ways, could be summarized in one heart-rending cry, "For God's sake, love me!"

We are grateful for this validation of our own convictions and for the focus Dr. Malone's succinct summary of the need for love has given to our writing.

We offer you this book with the prayer that it will speak to whatever emptiness cries in your heart.

In one of its chapters you may see yourself. In the story of Susan, of Erling, of John, of Sally, of Richard, you may discover the love you've been looking for.

Above all, we want you once again to see Jesus, God's answer to your heart's cry for love.

One

THE LONGING
for LOVE

The longing has never left me. I (Erling) have always wanted to experience my father's love. He was a distant man, as difficult to reach as the ever-receding horizon of the Dakotas.

The grain elevator he managed stood stark and lonely as he himself, towering above the prairie land right next to the shining railroad tracks.

Those Great Northern tracks tied our little village to the world of Minnesota in the east and to Montana in the west, to the vast fields of grain and the remote little towns of the Dakotas. The railroad was the vital artery that brought coal to heat our houses in the subzero winters and carried away our wonderful durum wheat to the great flour mills of the Twin Cities in the summer.

Summers in North Dakota were blisteringly hot. When the railroad station master wasn't around, my friends Mayo and Clem and I would "borrow" the handcar he used whenever he had to go short distances on down the track to make minor repairs on the railroad bed. We used it to get to the creek two and a half miles west of town, where there was enough water to swim and cool off.

What a sense of exhilaration came as we flew along that slightly downhill track, bending forward and backward, two of us in rhythm with the hand pumper, getting up to tremendous speeds of 15 miles an hour, the wind cooling our perspiring bodies under the burning sun. On the way back we got sweaty all over again, but the stolen excursion to the creek was worth it.

That railroad was part of my life, but mainly because it was part of my father's life, as was the Great Western Grain Company elevator that stood by the side of the tracks. The elevator was a large, four-part storage building rising many stories high above our town. Painted red, it could be seen across the flat land from a dozen miles away on a clear day.

At harvest time hundreds of farmers brought their grain to town, to the elevator, for sale or storage. In the early days they came in horse-drawn wagons, later in their Ford or Chevy trucks.

In a little, cluttered office in a separate building a short distance away, across 20 feet of wooden walkway, sat my father, waiting for each load of grain to arrive. Prince Albert tobacco smoldered in his pipe and filled the room with its sweet-acrid smoke.

In the winter the office was burning hot, heated by a glowing pot-bellied stove with an insatiable appetite for coal. My father kept it well fed and burning red between his trips into the bitter cold outside every time he had to sell coal. Summer or winter there was never any rest for the manager of the elevator.

But summer during harvest was the busiest time of all. Then my normally reserved father became more remote than usual.

In the summer, careful not to get in his way, I would come quietly into the office and watch him work. He was not a big man, but rather short and wiry with a red handlebar mustache. He hardly sat still for a minute. Up and down, in and out of the office he ran, constantly on the move.

People would say of him, "That Ole Wold sure is a worker! Smart, too. He gives you a fair price for your load, but never a penny more, or a penny less."

As soon as he saw a truck approaching, he ran out of the office and made sure that the truck coming up the short incline was centered on the platform, which was really a scale.

He weighed the truck and then climbed up on its high "box" to run a thin cylindrical steel tube through its contents to the bottom of the truck bed. When the tube hit the bottom, it automatically sealed itself, and, when pulled out of the grain, it provided a sample of the truck's contents.

The sample was poured into a nearby bucket and stirred. Exactly one pound of the grain was weighed out. That one pound would go into a separator, a machine that shook the grain violently, separating the good whole kernels from the undesirable broken bits, the weed seeds and the chaff. These rejected pieces were thrown away and burned.

The farmer was paid only for the whole kernels, and that one-pound sample told the story of the whole load. If the rejected pieces were 10 percent of the sample, then 10 percent of the truckload was discounted. Only 90 percent of the load was paid for.

This testing was crucial, and the farmer waited for my father's verdict, knowing that the farmer's income for the year waited on Ole Wold's decision.

There my father stood, all of the laughter and joking among the men stopped during that anxious moment of waiting. With their worn bib overalls, grimy hats sweaty from the heat of the harvest sun, scuffed work shoes, sunburned faces with white foreheads, dusty beards, hands stained and callused, these were thrifty, hardworking people who rose long before dawn to milk cows so they could get at their harvesting when the sun came up. The women and children were part of the whole enterprise and knew what a difference the price of grain meant for the whole family.

So they waited. The smell of grain and dust and sweat hung heavy in the summer air.

My father was judge and jury. Like God, I thought, he tests the evidence, makes the decision, pronounces the verdict.

I never heard anyone debate my father's judgment. Six percent, three percent, ten percent of their load thrown away, they accepted his word as final.

How my heart swelled with pride as I watched this stern man work! He seldom smiled, never laughed. Work was all he knew.

The verdict given, the front end of the truck was elevated so the load could cascade out through a floor grating into a large steel bin below.

This was the signal for me to follow the grain to its destination. For a little while I could enter my father's domain and become part of the creation he controlled.

With a flip of a switch he started hidden wheels turning, conveyor belts pulling, buckets lifting, and grain moving up to the very top of the elevator.

As fast as I could go, I would run up the narrow stairway around the inside wall of the elevator. Up, up to a single small room at the very top above the grain bins, where the only windows in the whole structure looked out on the world. To be at the top of the only "skyscraper" in the whole area, smelling the dusty mustiness of the dark inner chamber and seeing the wonder of the golden river of grain pouring into the bins below was to be really alive. The sound of the motors many stories down was muffled by the shushing of the cascading grain.

Danger added to the excitement. Only an eight-inch catwalk separated the bins of barley, rye, oats, and wheat. To get to the other side of the room at the top, I had to inch along those catwalks, totally frightened by the lure of the dark, dusty depths. I knew that if a bin were empty, I'd be killed by a fall; if it were partly filled, I might sink and suffocate or scream in vain for help. But the inviting windows drew me across with their promise of another view of my world.

This was my father's world, and my world of golden fields, gravel roads, winding rivers, and painted wooden houses. Our house, built by my father and his friends, was right next to the only church in the community. Even the tall steeple, which my father alone of all the men in the town had dared to climb when it needed a coat of paint, was dwarfed from my position at the top of the elevator.

This was my world, and my father seemed to me to be its "god."

Wasn't he absolutely essential to the life of the whole community? Didn't the economy of the town depend on those farmers below and the grain they brought to the elevator? And weren't they dependent on the Great Western Grain Company to buy their grain? And wasn't my father the agent of that company?

In my child's mind he was the most important man in town.

I could understand, I thought, why he was too busy to talk to people. He was too important.

Naturally, he was too busy to talk to me.

He never took a vacation or played games. At home he

ate in silence and went to bed, worn out from the day's labors.

How I admired him and longed for a word from him, a word that showed that I mattered in his life, that he admired even my fearless ascent into the dizzying and dangerous heights of the elevator. Just a word that would assure me that he loved me.

I soon figured out that the way to be close to him was to work alongside him. I knew that he needed help in the summer months unloading the coal from the railroad cars that were parked on the sidetrack next to the elevator. The coal had to be unloaded from the railroad cars and transferred to the large storage rooms adjoining the elevator and next to the tracks.

There was no mechanism to do this, no whirring wheels, no belts, no mechanical buckets. Everything had to be done by hand. Every piece of coal had to be lifted and transferred to the storage rooms by human effort.

The coal came in boxcars with four-feet-high boards across the doors. There were several of these boards, one upon the other, keeping the coal in the boxcar from running out. Each board had to be removed, one at a time from the top down, as layer after layer of coal was moved from the car to storage.

When I was 12 years old, I asked my father to let me shovel the coal. In my bib overalls, shirtless, feet encased in heavy boots, with work gloves protecting my hands, I worked a number of days every summer shoveling coal. Every morning when a boxcar was dropped off by the train I was there ready to unload it. A boxcar held 32 to 34 tons of coal. The hand shovel given to me by my father was called a "scoop." The scoop held about 25 pounds of coal.

I could unload a boxcar in one day if I worked at a furious pace. I would dig my way through the coal near the door down to the floor. Once down to the floor, I used a **U**-shaped mobile shovel on wheels, at least four times larger than the scoop.

With as much of a running start as I could get I would plow this "pusher" along the floor of the mountain of coal in the boxcar, whirl with it, and run with it, out the door and up the walkway to empty it into the storage room. With pounding heart and gasping breath, I went back and forth from boxcar to bin until the load had been transferred.

At noon, my father would appear at the boxcar. "Time for lunch," he'd say, and start walking home without so much as a backward glance to see if I were following.

Brushing off as much of the coal dust as I could, wiping my sooty boots, dropping my gloves, I ran after him, still pulling my shirt over my head.

We walked the three blocks in silence, speaking only when people greeted us on the street.

Farmers who had brought a load of grain in to town would stop him. "Thirty bushels to the acre this year," they'd say to him. "Not bad, huh, Ole?"

"Not bad, Paul," he'd say, "but too bad the mustard got into your fields." We'd walk on.

The rural mail carrier would be coming back to town. "The hail got a lot of Pete's crop," he might call out.

"Too bad," my father would say. "Pete's credit is not very good in town any more."

When we got home, lunch was ready. Beef and gravy, boiled potatoes, carrots from the garden, steamed and buttered. Homebaked bread.

"Are you tired, Erling?" mother would ask.

Without waiting for a reply she'd ask father, "He's not working too hard, is he, Ole? He's just a boy, you know."

"Work never hurt anybody," my father would say. "Make a man out of him."

My father ate fast, and when he was done, that was the end of lunch.

One day, back at work, I fainted from heat exhaustion. The grown men who had the job before me had taken more than a day to a empty a boxcar.

I was determined to show my father that I could work harder and faster than anyone else had ever worked. I thought then that I *felt* his approval, but I don't recall his ever saying it. I wanted him to *say* it. I wanted so much to know that he loved me.

The cry of my heart was, "For God's sake, love me, father! Love me!"

The hidden hunger for an expression of his love has stayed with me all these years. As a child, I couldn't articulate my need. It was hidden in the recesses of my spirit. But I know the need was there, partly satisfied by my mother and my brothers and sisters. But father remained remote, distant. If working hard did not make one worthy of his love, what did?

Gradually I let go of the drive to please him. I reached out to others to fill my need for love. Friends, academic achievement, vocation, and, later, marriage and family made me forget the early ache for my father's love and approval.

Or so I thought. Then why do I still feel that ache whenever I think of those long-ago summer days of my childhood?

We are born with an inexhaustible appetite for love and closeness. A baby drinks its fill at its mother's breast and, satiated, relaxes and sleeps.

Just a little while later the baby awakes, crying as if it had never eaten before in its life!

Gradually, as the months and years pass, it will begin to understand that food will be there when it's needed, and the hunger anxiety will be reduced.

The need for love is a hunger that must be satisfied in childhood by the significant adults in one's life.

As a constant counterpoint to all of life's themes, the cry is there from the time of our birth, "For God's sake, love me!"

Two

OUR NEED for LOVE

I (Marge) discovered that same aching emptiness when I was at a desert place leading a group of people in a spiritual retreat. My assignment was to create an environment for spiritual renewal for the 30 retreatants.

The setting was perfect: a Franciscan monastery in the desert, with warm winter sun in the day and cold desert nights. The dry terrain with its struggling flora appeared a suitable environment for people whose lives felt dry and barren. The small, cell-like rooms of the monastery seemed designed to strip away the veneers of everyday living. The seductions of the commercial world were not audible in the remoteness of the desert hills.

In the conversations around the dinner table that first night, as an undercurrent to the usual exchange of personal information, work-related topics, and the recounting of the latest jokes, I sensed tiredness, some depression, and a groping for relatedness.

Knowing that these were busy people, high-achieving professionals, trained in left-brained ways of thinking and behaving, I knew that I had to engage them in some activity that would "lower their center of gravity."

Too much mental activity without an opportunity to express feelings makes us top-heavy. We become dry and sterile, unable to experience the joy of God's presence.

I had brought 25 pounds of modeling clay with me. At the first group session the next morning, I handed each person a good-sized chunk of the clay and told them that they were to go off by themselves to find their own solitary places and to let their hands work the clay.

"This activity," I explained, "will help to free you from the inhibitions created in you by the responsibilities of your workaday world and permit you to become like children again. Do you remember what Jesus said? 'Unless you become like little children, you will never enter the kingdom of heaven.' You're here to revive your faith-life, and your 'adult' can be a stumbling block to faith."

By this time the clay had made the rounds, and some were holding it rather carefully but taking tentative pokes into it.

"How long is it since you've had clay in your hands?" I asked.

"I think it was when I was five," someone said.

Someone else made a joke. "Actually I keep some in my office and play with it every day." Laughter.

Another man picked up on that. "No, I really did play with clay just a week ago when they had father's night at my son's preschool. If I remember right, we all felt kind of silly, like I'm feeling now. But our kids were there, so we pretended it was great fun."

"Today," I told them, "this is not for fun, although I hope you will find it an enjoyable experience. I want you to take this as a serious opportunity for spiritual insight."

I explained that they were not to think consciously

about making some "thing," but simply to meditate on the clay, remembering the words of the prophet Jeremiah, that we are clay in the potter's hands (Jer. 18:1-6). "Let your hands think for you," I said, "and let the Spirit shape the clay."

With rather sheepish grins and self-conscious comments they left the meeting room to find their own place for solitary reflection.

Soon I could hear sounds of clay being slapped and pounded. I relaxed. They were taking the exercise seriously.

Alone in the meeting room, I rather absentmindedly picked up a handful of clay. The moist chunk of earth was cool and inviting. My hands began to work it. Lost in my own thoughts, I soon forgot about the others.

What does the Potter have to tell me? I wondered.

My hands kept smoothing the ball of clay until it was perfectly round and without crease or blemish.

A sense of satisfaction warmed me. Certainly my life was full and complete, I thought. I had come full circle in my life. I reflected on the fact that my children were grown and educated, my husband and I still found life together exciting and full, and I had satisfying and worthwhile work to do.

Even as I reflected, I felt something happening to the clay that I had no conscious intention of doing.

The very thing that I had told the others to do—to let go and to let their hands do their thinking for them—was happening to me. My right thumb was pushing its way down into the center of the clay, hollowing out a smooth, empty space in the middle of my lovely, perfect ball.

When it was hollowed out, an even stranger thing happened. Without disturbing the empty space at its core, my hand carefully replaced the clay over it, and once more the outside of the clay looked perfectly whole and smooth. No one but me could ever have guessed that there was a hole, an empty place, tucked away in the middle of my clay.

I shivered as the Spirit seemed to be saying to me, "Don't ever be deceived. No matter who the person is, no matter how smooth and self-sufficient he or she seems to be, there is always an empty place inside that can be satisfied only when God is permitted to move into it."

My concentration was shattered when I heard the others returning from their hour of reflection. They came into the room carrying various objects made out of the clay, which they held carefully all the while they were deprecating and ridiculing these personal sculptures.

I asked them if they were willing to go into small groups and share what had happened to them in their hour alone. They appeared eager to do that.

In their little gatherings around the room, they talked animatedly, taking turns describing their experiences.

I walked around, listening to some of their stories of their feelings and of how the shapes had emerged out of their hands.

One young man displayed a rather elaborate sculpture. "I haven't played with clay since I was in kindergarten," he said, apologetically. "And I'm sure no artist, but for the past year I've felt as though I've been out of my depth in an ocean of depression and going down for the third time."

His sculpture was of a head with the nose just above some choppy waves. The only other object above the water was a large hand reaching for help.

"My wife left me a year ago," he said. "My whole world fell apart. I couldn't tell anyone about it for fear that I would lose my job. My boss doesn't believe in divorce. Anyway,

I didn't think anyone cared to hear about my pain. At the same time I wanted to yell for help and have someone grab my hand and pull me out before I went down for the last time."

The group was quiet. Then someone spontaneously reached out and held his hand. Someone else reached over and gave him a big hug and that broke the ice.

Unashamedly, he began to cry. "I've felt so alone," he sobbed.

I remembered something Mother Teresa of Calcutta had said, that she has come more and more to realize that *being unwanted* is the worst disease any human being can experience. Other diseases have medicines and cures, but without a loving heart to love them, the victims of this disease can never be cured.

I wandered over to another group. There an older man was talking about his sculpture. His clay had shaped a bird, quite a realistic figure of a dove. But the bird had only one wing, outstretched, beating the air, feathers visible, a perfect wing. But only one wing.

"I've always wanted my life to take off, to really 'fly,'" he said, "and I've done some noteworthy things. I've achieved enough to satisfy most people, I guess. But somehow I've been afraid to really take off, to risk giving up security and what I have now, to face the future without a safety net. I really feel like a bird with only one wing. I'm afraid to get out there and do something that people might think is crazy and unacceptable. Working with this clay made me realize that one of the things I've always wanted to do is study art. But here I am, in my 50s, in a profession with a lot of security."

Where did this man get the need to do what others approve of instead of following his own dream? Who had given him such a need to find approval? Had love been withdrawn when he "got out of line?"

Tragically, we may dig hollows in our own psyches. We use the shovel others hand us and bury our dreams rather than risk moving into unknown territory. Terrified at the thought of losing the love of others, we play it safe and never learn to develop our own wings.

Still holding my own smooth ball of clay in my hands, feeling its deceptive exterior and subconsciously pondering the hidden hollow in its center, I moved to another group.

There a well-dressed woman in her 30s was talking. She had added two stick figures to her clay sculpture. They were made out of the stems of some of the desert plants. Between the figures rose a thick, impenetrable, fortress-like barrier made out of all of the clay except some she had used for the base.

"I'm afraid to get close to anyone," she was saying. "I'm beginning to put up a barrier between me and everyone else. Whenever I trust people, I always end up betrayed. Working through the bitterness of these past years has not been easy."

Her bitterness stemmed most recently from the betrayal she had experienced at the hands of the people with whom she worked. She had accepted a job on the strength of a promise that she would be promoted within a year to a much better paying, more responsible position.

Three years passed. Her employer's son was brought into the business and given the position promised to her. He had only two years of college, while she had her M.B.A. And he had none of her experience.

"I swallowed my disappointment," she told the group, "and I again accepted the promise that the next turn would be mine. But when the next opening came, it was a friend of my boss's son who got the job."

A long pause. Then she straightened her back and went on. "I'm sorry," she said, "I should be talking about more cheerful things. Nobody wants to hear my sob story. But I'm tired of pretending, of having to wear a mask of cheerfulness, when I feel so angry inside."

Isn't that exactly one of the problems? Doesn't the need to appear cheerful, forced to wear a mask that hides our real feelings, isn't that part of our emptiness?

Where can we find intimacy, a real closeness to other people, if we fear that closeness will lead to a betrayal of our love and trust?

In the desert air, the monastery bell rang out its invitation to lunch. With a promise that there would be further time for reflection on our clay experience, the group broke up with hugs, assurances of love, and continued animated sharing.

Alone in the room, I decided to skip lunch and to think more about my own "sculpture." What did that empty space in my clay mean?

I had no particular needs that I knew of. My life truly was full of meaning, and filled with the love of many significant persons. Why had my thumb hollowed out that empty space?

As I turned my clay around and around, like a "worry stone" or a prayer object, I began to sense its meaning. *Wasn't the hole there to remind me that part of my life must always be kept deliberately empty?*

A life can become too full, I thought. Even all those good things and loving people can crowd out the place that must be kept empty for God.

In his book *Clowning in Rome*, Henri Nouwen describes the large empty churches scattered throughout the busy weekday world that is the city of Rome. In the crowded markets and business areas, the churches are sacred spaces, usually empty, and kept that way for God. Without them there would be only shops and stalls, offices and conference rooms, buying and selling, cash-flow statements and bottom lines.

Without that empty space in my clay, it would just be a solid lump of smooth dirt, I thought. Without an empty space in me, I might forget that only God can satisfy my deepest needs.

In my hands the clay began to take on its own warmth. The empty space hidden inside gave it a secret meaning all its own. No one else might ever know it was there, but *I* knew. It would always remind me that God, who had created that secret space in the clay of our lives, meant it to be filled only with God's own love. It must never be filled with other loves.

Augustine, Christian convert and writer about God in the fifth century, made his now famous observation that God has made us for God's own self, and our hearts are restless until they find their rest in God.

To put anyone or anything else in the "God-shaped vacuum" is to fill it with an idol. And idolatry only leads to increasing emptiness.

If one has a fear of that empty space inside of oneself, it may mean that one is running away from God.

I thought of Jean, who experienced panic whenever she had to be alone. The moment the door closed behind the last child leaving for school, she felt like running out of the house. She couldn't stand to see her husband off on the plane, because the moment the plane taxied down the runway she panicked and wanted to run after him.

The thought of being alone with herself without anything to do terrified her. She exhausted herself walking up and down shopping malls, keeping her house spotless, watching television programs that she didn't even like. Everything she did was designed, however unconsciously, to keep her from confronting the emptiness inside herself.

The words of a friend revealed Jean to herself. Eating lunch one day at a shopping-mall restaurant, her friend commented that it was so nice to have a place like the mall where every bit of space was filled with things to look at. "You don't even have to buy anything," she said. "It makes you feel good just to walk around and look at all the things."

Jean saw herself like the mall—a big empty space trying to get filled up with things!

When I meet people like Jean, I'm reminded of a movie about a woman who lived a life devoid of dreams or hopes. In the movie the woman said that she loved driving in Los Angeles, because one could get on the freeways and drive all day and never get anywhere!

We will go to great lengths to fill that longing emptiness inside. To escape, to run away from the only One who can fill it with ultimate satisfaction—that's our goal. The trick is to fill time with whatever will distract one from the fearful void.

For Jean, the mall held that promise.

For Erling, work was the answer, at least for a while. Intensive work dulled the longing for a father's love, while at the same time proving his acceptability to his father.

How many men and women today are trying to fill their emptiness with work? Keeping busy, running from plane to plane, carrying our suitbags and attaché cases, we will discuss with any stranger our latest achievements and believe that we have satisfied our empty longing for a meaningful relationship and love.

In the evening, with the day's work done, the emptiness

of a hotel room after a lonely restaurant dinner is an unbearable prospect, so it's down to the "lounge," for loud music and more strangers to try to converse with, hoping in the loud laughter and alcohol to find surcease from the emptiness crying within.

But let's not be misled into thinking that uncommunicative parents are the cause of all of our empty places.

I, for instance, knew from the time I was born that I was wanted and loved. My parents had lost their first two babies before any of the rest of us were born. When my older brother and I came along just one year apart, my parents felt that God had given them their two babies back again. Every one of their children (all eight of us) were told that we were wanted and loved. We knew it! We were hugged, praised, played with, encouraged, admired.

But, in spite of all of that childhood love, I still felt an emptiness inside. The aching void became especially painful when one little brother died. I was ten years old at the time, and the loneliness inside, even in the midst of a large, loving family, was a private agony to be suffered in silence.

Erling filled his emptiness with sports, activities, and, of course, work.

I filled mine with school. Studies, learning, achieving, getting good grades filled my life. The more I was praised for my A's, the more I studied, assuming that was the way to get enough love and meaning to stop the hollow echo in my empty spirit.

At the end of my senior year in high school I realized that there were other ways to fill the emptiness. There was more to life than books and grades. I discovered boys and dates, dances, proms, parties. The search for fun and good times dominated my life.

Dancing became my "idol." I thought I couldn't live

without dancing. Even after graduation, working at a bank in downtown Chicago, I managed to go dancing with someone at least three or four times a week. This was the era of the big bands, and famous ballrooms like the Aragon and Trianon were bright spots in the Chicago of the Depression.

Still the emptiness.

You can add your story to all of the above.

How are you trying to fill that hole in the middle of the clay of your being, that space shaped for God? What crowds your days, exhausting you to sleep at night?

Perhaps nothing grips your interest or focuses your attention long enough to satisfy the aching hunger in you. You may be one of the millions who must dull the sobbing of your spirit with sedatives, with alcohol, with some chemical substance that numbs your brain into believing that the emptiness isn't there.

Take heart. The emptiness is there for a purpose.

At the creation of the cosmos, says the narrator in the first chapter of the Bible, everything was without form and void. Chaos reigned. Nothing had shape or meaning. It was like driving through the fog or wandering in a dream that has no form. Or walking through an endless mall. Or driving on a freeway to nowhere. The earth was without form and void.

But, hallelujah, the Spirit of God was brooding over the face of the deep! That brooding Spirit is the life-changing breath of God waiting until the time is ripe to give shape to the chaos, the unformed waiting emptiness that is the womb of all creation.

Your emptiness, my emptiness, Erling's wanting, and all of the cries molded into the clay at the retreat are the stuff from which God can create new life.

The void is the space in which God can be born in you.

It's the place where God hears our individual cries, "For God's sake, love me!" and is shaping the answer that each one of us is waiting for.

Three

LOVE'S ANSWER

Why that emptiness? Why the insatiable hunger for love?

Even with all the love in the world—of parents, of spouse, of peers—why do we still feel empty and void at times, in fact, at the least expected time?

One of America's best-known comediennes, Joan Rivers, was quoted by an interviewer for the in-flight magazine *Mainliner* as saying, "I see life as—nobody is happy. Nobody is comfortable. Nobody is at home, anywhere. People don't know where they belong. So my comedy is about that state, about where we are all at."

We observe that all religions describe in some way the separation that exists between the Creator and humans.

Zanahary, say the Malagasy, created the earth and all people in it and then rejected them because they displeased him. So he went away to live in a far place, never again to have contact with the human race.

Unkulunkulu, the Zulu believe, must be appeased and offered gifts to make him accept his alienated creatures.

Yahweh, says the writer of Genesis, found the people of this earth so repulsive because of their sins that he was sorry he had ever made them and sent a flood to destroy them all, saving only one family to give the race another chance.

Our dilemma goes back to the garden of creation, says the Bible. We were made to be like God, designed in God's image.

The temptation to be *more* than just the image of God overpowered the human race. The urge to take God's place was too much to resist. The hiss of the serpent has always whispered in our hearts, "Become as powerful as God. Become God!"

Yielding to the blandishments of the tempter to disobey God, we are alienated from our Creator. Instead of walking with God in the beauty and freedom of the garden, we are driven out to make our way in the deserts and among the brambles and thistles of the world.

Alienation from God and from each other has carved that empty space in the deep recesses of our beings.

Our deepest need is to know once again fellowship with our Maker, to be assured that God still loves us, still loves *me*.

No one else can cure that ache, appease that appetite, fill that emptiness.

God knows that, and God alone knows the exact shape of that love vacuum in our hearts. And God has revealed that shape to us. Its shape is a cradle, designed to receive a baby. Fashioned before the world began in the mind of God and given human form in the womb of a virgin named Mary, the baby was called Jesus.

Jesus assumed the shape of the vacuum in our hearts. God's love came down in the shape of Jesus to fill our emptiness.

How is it possible for us to comprehend the power of a divine love that would subject itself voluntarily to the pains and limitations of human flesh in a plunging descent from glory?

Can love be that powerful?

In 1986 the mighty Kilauea erupted on the island of Hawaii. Even the television videotapes of its fiery explosion were awesome. We watched the hot lava pour fountain-like out of the volcano's mouth, boiling up from the heart of the island, many tons per second, aflame with heat at 2000° Fahrenheit.

Fire fighters were pictured with their hoses shooting puny little streams of water in a futile effort to cool its flow.

Chewing its way through rock, eating up highways, consuming houses, the lava sizzled its way into the ocean, creating new acres of island and changing the landscape forever.

At night its glory illuminated the entire sky in a spectacular display of light.

The number of tourists doubled. Everyone wanted to see it.

What a vivid picture of the pent-up love of God pouring out of the very heart of the cosmos! When the Creator decided to move into our world in a mighty eruption of love, that act forever changed the course of all human history and of our own personal histories.

Martin Luther stumbled over words trying to explain the love of God. He said it was like an ocean so vast that it has no shoreline and no bottom. What would he have said could he have seen Kilauea?

Luther saw God's loving passion as being so immense that it is as endless as God is. God's love has nothing to fence it in. It started to erupt even before time began.

Jesus, child of God, the lamb of God's love, was there with God when the foundations of the world were laid.

You can sense the edge of God's pain when the price of reconciliation with us became evident. To let that love of God explode into our world cost the life of God's "love child," who volunteered to pay the price with his own blood.

Nothing in the Scriptures can shake one up as violently as that realization.

Everything that we learn about the cosmos—and so much is being discovered in our age—only humbles us the more. A famed astrophysicist, Dr. William Kaufman, lectured at California Lutheran University, where we teach. He rightly pointed out that it is impossible for the human mind to conceive of limitless space. "We cannot, no matter how hard we try, we cannot think of space without some kind of boundary, as though, perhaps, it's enclosed in a big plastic bag," he said. "To imagine something without a beginning or an ending is beyond our capabilities as finite creatures."

Yet God is the one "who is, and who was, and who is to come," the Alpha and the Omega, the first and the last (Rev. 1:8).

Even Paul the apostle, who spent much time alone in the wilderness being taught by the Spirit of God, could not fathom a Creator whose love knows no limits. At the end of his most profound writing about Jesus in the first three chapters of the letter to the Ephesians, he soars to ecstatic heights:

> For this reason I kneel before the Father, from whom his whole family in heaven and on earth derives its name. I pray that out of his glorious riches he may strengthen you with power through his Spirit in your inner being, so that Christ may dwell in your hearts by faith. And I pray that you, being rooted and established in love, may have power, together with

all saints, to grasp how wide and long and high and deep is the love of Christ, and to know this love that surpasses knowledge—that you may be filled to the measure of all the fullness of God.

(Eph. 3:14-19)

The very word *love* triggers Paul's spirit to add that God is able to do "immeasurably more than all we ask or imagine." Paul seems to pile eternally high mountain ranges upon mountain ranges upon mountain ranges, trying to lift us into the realm of the inexpressible.

The love of God is something a child can sing about: "Jesus loves me, this I know." At the same time, love floods the universe with its inexhaustible glory.

Ultimately the love of God cannot be described. It can only be experienced.

Although Kilauea contains in its bowels a continuous active lake of molten lava, it normally is caged for centuries in its earthen prison. But its destiny is to burst the restraints of its confinement, and it has gushed forth some 44 times in this century.

The entire being of God is a burning volcano of love, and the Scriptures picture history as the story of that love, seeking, plunging, veering, dashing, enveloping, taking detours and side roads, making its own highway to its destination.

Love was erupting from the heart of God when the cries of God's people went up out of Egypt: "The Israelites groaned in their slavery and cried out, and their cry for help because of their slavery went up to God. God heard their groaning and he remembered . . ." (Exod. 2:23-24).

God's saving love brought them out of their bondage, across the sea and through the wilderness, fed them with manna, gave them water in the desert, and brought them into their promised land.

Israel could never forget that the love of God for them was the centerpiece of their national life. It anchored their whole existence. They might stray from God's love. They might violate it. But they could never deny it.

The prophet Isaiah sang about that supportive and restoring love of God, "But now, this is what the Lord says—

Fear not, for I have redeemed you;
   I have summoned you by name; you are mine.
When you pass through the waters, I will be with you;
   and when you pass through the rivers, they will not
   sweep over you.
When you walk through the fire, you will not be burned;
   the flames will not set you ablaze. . . .
Since you are precious and honored in my sight,
   and because I love you. . . ."

(Isa. 43:1-2,4)

Yet all of these pre-Jesus outbursts of love are like candles in the sunlight. They pale and fade in the exploding glory of God's love in Christ.

Jesus, the baby in the manger, son of Mary, is incarnate love. Into the darkness of our cradling world, the child is born.

Incarnate: "The Word became flesh and made his dwelling among us. We have seen his glory, the glory of the One and Only Son" (John 1:14).

Now we're right back to that incomprehensible reality of God taking human form and living among us. We're back at the astrophysicist's limitless God of limitless space.

We travel in jet planes at altitudes 37,000 or more feet, and we cannot see a single human being on the earth below. We don't even have to be that high off the ground. Even at 5000 feet we see no human beings with our naked eyes. At that height we can see our houses and our barns, our cars and our trains, but we humans ourselves are not visible.

From any point in space we do not exist.

We war, we fight, we murder, we rape, we defile the air, the land, and the water. We make crosses and kill each other.

Why would God choose to become human? To become, not a powerful human, but a helpless human? A baby, one of the most helpless of all creatures.

The only conceivable answer is "love."

We can understand that, can't we?

If you care enough, you will even choose to die for the ones you love. Remember the four Maryknoll missionary women, three nuns and one laywoman? Their raped, mutilated, and murdered bodies gave anguished evidence of the love that brought them to El Salvador.

They, too, had a choice. They could have stayed in the safety and comfort of their own land, but instead they chose to live among the people whose cries they had heard, cries which drew them to that war-torn country.

Missionaries have died, soldiers have died, patriots have died—responding to the physical and spiritual oppressions of other human beings. Parents have died to save their children, and children have died to save their parents.

Yet, what is our love compared to the love of God?

If missionaries can go to people they have never seen and give their lives for them, cannot the God who formed my "inmost being," who "knit me together in my mother's womb" come to live among us? God surely knows us and loves us. Space and distance and our invisibility are not a problem with God. In the secret places of our being nothing is hidden. "Where can I go from your Spirit? Where can I flee from your presence?" (Ps. 139:7).

The question is not whether God knows and can love us. The question is whether we want to know and love God.

The baby, God incarnate, is the Word of God, the explanation of God. The infant Jesus by his very presence is saying, "This is what God is like; this is what God's love is like."

God is everything we love.

Doesn't everyone love a baby? Don't they coo their way into our hearts? Don't they use every part of their being, their voices, their body language, their eyes, to try to attract us? Don't they struggle to be absorbed into our arms and our hearts? Don't they show their vulnerability in being needed? Every baby is all of this.

In Jesus, God is all of this.

Can you see now the brilliance of the love of God?

Does the magnificent display of stars in the heavens make us experience the love of God? They've been there forever, and human beings have both taken them for granted as a part of natural phenomena and have also marveled at the mysteries of their origins and destiny. While the profusion and mystery of the stars may cause some to fall down and worship, they cannot tell us that their Maker cares about them or us.

Would we experience the love of God if God had come to us as a benevolent ruler, marshaling armies and economies and academies to make us all powerful and rich and smart?

Obviously we can list all of the ways humans have pictured their gods. Although the anthropomorphic antics of the long-forgotten "gods" on Mount Olympus both fascinated and repelled the ancient Greeks and Romans, they never won their love. They were never portrayed as being anything but jealous and vindictive teasers of earthlings. Gods have been pictured as warriors, drunkards, rapists, benefactors, sages, impregnators of the earth, and as fertility goddesses.

But we who know Jesus can sing, "Love came down

at Christmas," because God came to us revealed in the most lovable and loving form possible, a baby.

Babies have a way of taking over our lives.

Kilauea's lava flow inexorably takes over whatever territory it wants. It makes demands on the island. Its priorities move to the top of Hawaii's agenda.

Ask any couple what happened to their home when baby arrived. The baby set the agenda for the day—and for the night! Meal schedules are altered to conform to baby's feeding times. Sleep patterns are changed to fit the baby's schedule.

Baby Jesus, love incarnate, came to change the human agenda. The good news that God is love and that God loves us was moved to the top of the list of time's priorities.

All human endeavors, structured in terms of intellect and commerce, of war and achievement, of hierarchies and of being "number one," received a new format for living and behaving.

Jesus, when he grew to adulthood, went about doing good.

He had everything against him in his lifetime. His principles were against those of his society. The religious system opposed him, because it had become just that, a system, and not the ongoing revelation of God's love. Hierarchies controlled the system.

For Jesus, the agenda was to demonstrate the love of God. He healed many, even some who didn't thank him for their healing. He drained himself for others. The powerless were lifted up. The poor followed him. He spoke words of forgiveness and proclaimed forgiveness as the ultimate demonstration of God's love.

No wonder they said of those who followed his way that they "turned the world upside down."

Like Kilauea lighting the night sky and the entire countryside with its flaming lava, Jesus comes as the "light of the world" (John 9:5). Love always brightens the world. Look at the faces of people in love. The sparkle in their eyes reveals the glowing fire within.

The darkness that Jesus illumines is the darkness of sin. He reminds us that there is a law for living that will remove the darkness of sin. "Love your neighbor as yourself" is the answer to biting and devouring one another (Gal. 5:14-15).

In these past decades our government has engaged in activities that have had to be hidden under a cloak of darkness. This has always resulted in shame and disgrace to many people and to our nation as a whole. What is done in the light does not need to be exposed. The wonder of the light of Jesus, John says, is that no one can snuff it out (John 1:5).

The light of God made known to us through the loving deeds of Jesus continues to lighten our darkness.

God's love motivates people to fight for justice, to feed the hungry, and to care for the homeless. Check the records of charitable giving in our country and note that the major share is given by church and synagogue people.

The most impelling reality of the lava flow is that it burns away all of the barriers in its path. Nothing in our world can stop it until it reaches its destination. Those licking flames instantly melt everything they touch—rock, steel, houses, walls.

The Bible says that God abhors everything evil. Evil cannot stand in the presence of love.

The baby Jesus is not among us to be cooed at, to be cute, or even to grow up to be the great model for human living, although he is that. The ultimate reason why he, who was in the form of God, "emptied himself," becoming human, has a much more profound expression of love. "And being found in appearance as a man, he humbled himself and became obedient to death—even death on a cross!" (Phil. 2:8). The love of God, poured down out of the flaming center of God's own nature, chose the cross as the means for destroying all obstacles to that love.

What a tragedy that people in Hawaii had to leave their homes, their memorabilia, their land. What a tragedy that the Son of God had to die on a cross! But that's why Jesus came.

Like the lava finding its way down to the sea, choosing its own paths, letting nothing stop it, Jesus went to the cross. "Out of my sight, Satan!" he rebuked Peter, when Peter tried to stop him (Matt. 16:23).

The cross was his destiny.

The tempter, the devil, had seduced the human race into rebellion against God's love. That rebellion had separated us from God (Genesis 3).

In our helpless condition, when we were powerless to change our situation, the extent of God's love was revealed.

God made the first move toward reconciliation. Instead of demanding our death as a payment for our sin, God let Jesus die in our place, destroying death in the process.

Since the children have flesh and blood, he too shared in their humanity so that by his death he might destroy him who holds the power of death—that is, the devil—and free those who all their lives were held in slavery by their fear of death.
(Heb. 2:14-15)

As the lava carries everything with it into the sea, so the love of God, poured out on the cross, carries our sins with it into the depths of the ocean of that love, and the place where they disappear washes over them, and they are remembered no more. They are buried and gone. Praise God!

Can you imagine it? The lava flow creates a new world. As it hardens on the submerged beach, it forms new land, and the law says that the new land belongs to everyone.

The glory of the God-love lies in the new world it gives us *now*.

Didn't Jesus promise that if we live and believe in him, we will never die? Didn't the apostle Paul write that upon us, now, the end of the ages has already come? Doesn't his letter to the Ephesians affirm that we have a dual citizenship, on earth and in heaven?

As we live in the love of God, the Spirit invites us to joy and exuberance and dancing. The early Christians, so taken by Jesus, threw their lives recklessly against the future. The music of their love still cascades through the ages.

God, the eternal source of extraordinary love, has answered our cry, "For God's sake, love me!"

Four

FALLING
in LOVE

Kim waited until all the rest of the class had left the room. She was an older student, and we often chatted after class. This time she could hardly wait until the last student was gone.

"Guess what!" she said, her eyes sparkling and excitement alive in her voice.

"What? Tell me quick!" I urged, responding to her excitement.

"Marge, you aren't going to believe this, but Sarah's in love!"

I could understand her excitement. Sarah, Kim's sister, is bright and articulate, well established in her profession, a political activist, and committed to reaching some heady career goals. I had met Sarah when I was working in another position and knew her to be a very powerful woman.

I said, yes, it *was* hard to believe.

Kim continued. "I can hardly stand to be around her now! All she talks about is this guy. She used to know him in high school about 15 years ago when he was going out with her girlfriend. Now he's moved to a place not too far from Sarah's house. Of course, he broke up with her friend a long time ago, but they still keep in touch, and she told him to look Sarah up."

The words tumbled over one another in Kim's enthusiastic telling of her sister's story.

"So he called her and asked her out to dinner, and they stayed in the restaurant talking for three hours. And she fell in love and he wants her to marry him and everybody's telling her to slow down, take it easy, and give it time. She says she knows she should wait, but she doesn't want to. My mother's been praying for her to find someone for a long time, but now even my mother says she didn't think Sarah would ever fall in love this hard!"

Anybody who's ever been in love can understand Sarah's response. In fact, we had written about that feeling in our book, *Bible Readings for Couples* (Augsburg, 1984):

We're finally married. It was a long time happening. I met you such a long time before we got together. Or so it seemed.

It was love at first sight with me. I remember so vividly falling into your eyes, tumbling end over end into their depths. Now my dreams are consummated.

"Be close," says God. "Be closer to one another than to anyone else in the whole world." I have to practice this daily, leaving parents, job, children, and hobbies. To give my mate top priority demands more than I am by nature willing to give. But the closeness we feel when I do is worth the effort. I'm glad God created us to be one flesh.

Closeness means opening up to you, letting you in on my hidden self, making myself vulnerable to you. Sometimes I'm afraid you might think me dumb, foolish or evil when I reveal myself, but that's the risk I have to take to insure continuing closeness. I try to trust you that much.

And it means that I will "pleasure" you. No other physical delight can touch making love. The touching, the caressing, the ecstasy all add to the richness of "cleaving" to each other.

Falling in love. The most uncommon, common human experience. It spins us around in a dizzying revolution of everything we are. Perspectives are altered; commitments are rearranged.

"She can't talk about anything but this guy!"

That statement describes what happens when one falls in love with Jesus. Christianity is not a theology, but a relationship.

We sense this obsession in the life of the apostle Paul. "For me to live is Christ!" he cried, and dashed around the world of his day, telling everyone about his newfound love. He wrote letters to both individuals and groups to help them catch his passion. "May I never boast except in the cross of our Lord Jesus Christ, through which the world has been crucified to me, and I to the world" (Gal. 6:14). The radical re-formation of Paul's whole life is in that statement.

And Sarah's life will never be the same again. If she makes the ultimate commitment to her newfound love, it means he will be the only romantic love in her life from that time on.

Paul knew what this kind of commitment could mean. "What is more," he wrote to his friends in the city of Philippi, "I consider everything a loss compared to the surpassing greatness of knowing Christ Jesus my Lord, for whose sake I have lost all things. I consider them rubbish, that I may gain Christ" (Phil. 3:7-8).

Everything Paul had been caught up in before he met the Lord on the way to Damascus (Acts 9:1-19) was reduced to "rubbish."

His zeal for the law, his passion to arrest and exterminate Christians, his working relationship with the power people of his country, his alliance with the high priest and friends of the authorities, his affiliation with his own "political" party, the Pharisees—all became rubbish, dung, garbage to be thrown away.

Sarah's mother was praying that she would fall in love, but not that much in love! But there's no way to fall in love halfway. You're either in love, or you're not in love.

When he met the risen Lord the apostle Paul, then Saul the Pharisee, was "still breathing out murderous threats against the Lord's disciples" and was heading for Damascus to arrest men and women "who belonged to the Way" that he "might take them as prisoners to Jerusalem."

In the midst of all of our commitments and activities, our relationships and plans, Jesus confronts us with himself and asks for our response to his love.

> But because of his great love for us, God, who is rich in mercy, made us alive with Christ even when we were dead in transgressions—it is by grace you have been saved. And God raised us up with Christ and seated us with him in the heavenly realms in Christ Jesus, in order that in the coming ages he might show the incomparable riches of his grace, expressed in his kindness to us in Christ Jesus.
>
> (Eph. 2:4-7)

It's got to be all or nothing, because God's commitment to us is nothing less than everything on earth and in heaven.

Sarah—independent, headstrong, fun-loving, intense Sarah—are you willing to make that much of a commitment to your love? And, in the spirit of the mutual submission the Scripture calls for (Eph. 5:21), is he willing to make that much of a commitment to you? How much of your own way will each one of you be willing to count as "rubbish" for the sake of the other?

That total commitment to each other was made particularly difficult for us when we, Erling and Marge, fell in love with each other. We were in college, he a senior and I a freshman.

When Erling asked me to marry him, I said no to him for several years in a row, because I had made a prior commitment to God to become a Bible teacher in another country. It seemed to me a betrayal of my prior love commitment to Jesus Christ to now say I would make a lifetime pledge to Erling. It took me five years to realize that marriage with Erling would only enhance both our ministries.

The apostle Paul had to make sense of his prior commitment to the God of the Torah and the people of Israel in the light of his new calling to become a witness for Christ to the Gentiles.

How could all that he was so fervent about before, the law, circumcision, separation from "unclean" foods, his zeal for the God of his ancestors—how could all of these things be reconciled with his love for the Christ of the Damascus way?

Paul was to learn that Jesus was the anointed one, the Messiah promised by the God of the Torah, the God of Abraham and Sarah, of Rebekah and Isaac, of Jacob and Rachel, and that the Torah was indeed the same law of love fulfilled in Jesus.

God was one and had led Paul's people out of slavery in Egypt, had guided them through the wilderness, fed them with manna in the desert, and led them into the promised land.

The same God had delivered Paul from the bondage of sin and led him through the wilderness of his own rebellion and into the promised land of grace and freedom.

When Paul discovered that the same God who had loved him and his people with "an everlasting love" was also the

Christ who loved him all the way to a cross, he understood that although the direction of his life had been changed, he was still walking with, and working for, the same God.

Falling in love requires a rearrangement of our priorities. Sarah, determined to become an executive in her multinational firm, would probably be required to move to another state—if not another country—in pursuit of her goals. Her newfound love, according to her sister, was committed to becoming the owner of the company for which he now worked.

Whose priorities would be rearranged? With their conviction that Christian marriage is a partnership of equals, they will have to engage in a mutual struggle to make their dreams come true.

Falling in love with Jesus Christ, however, does not mean a partnership arrangement with God. "Jesus is Lord!" was the first confession required of Christian disciples. That means Jesus is Lord of one's whole life, the entire agenda.

"I will show him how much he must suffer for my name," Jesus said about Paul to Ananias, the Lord's disciple at Damascus (Acts 9:16). The contract that comes with our "call" to discipleship is signed in Christ's own blood.

Later, in a letter to the Christians at Corinth, Paul would list all the things he had suffered in the fulfillment of his call to bring the gospel of God's love to the Gentiles.

I have worked harder, been in prison more frequently, been flogged more severely, and been exposed to death again and again. Five times I received from the Jews the forty lashes minus one. Three times I was beaten with rods, once I was stoned, three times I was shipwrecked, I spent a night and a day in the open sea, I have been constantly on the move. I have been in danger from rivers, in danger from bandits, in danger from my own countrymen, in danger from Gentiles; in danger in the city, in danger in the country, in danger at sea; and in danger from false brothers. I have labored and toiled and have often gone without sleep; I have known hunger and thirst and have often gone without food; I have been cold and naked. (2 Cor. 11:23-27)

Ah, the pains we will suffer for love! Sarah cannot eat or sleep. If the phone doesn't ring when he has promised to call, she tortures herself with visions of her own inadequacies, or with the possibilities that he may have been injured in an accident or met someone else or. . . . Then to be reunited and to learn that all of the suffering was for nothing is pure joy!

If we will suffer so much at the hands of another human, imagine what falling in love with God calls for!

The call to discipleship does not promise us a life of ease, even though that false promise is sometimes given to others who have never been called to suffer for the sake of Christ. Not everyone is called to the same calling, but Jesus did say that his followers would have to take up their cross and follow him (Mark 8:34).

No matter where the way of the cross takes us, God has promised to those who follow Jesus, both God's presence and God's faithfulness.

In this time of easy human divorce and unfaithfulness, the promise of Jesus that he will never leave us or forsake us is marvelous assurance.

We enter our human love relationship with that hope of faithfulness, convinced that our love will be different from those that dissolve with time. Our love will last, we reassure one another.

Sarah wants passionately to keep her love alive. The exciting ecstasy subordinates everything else. It obliterates some things that used to be primary in her life. Bertrand Russell said that he would gladly sacrifice the rest of his life if he could only find a few hours of joy.

Paul, falling in love with Jesus, was caught up in this same desire. In a cry that echoed from the depths of his being, he expressed the ultimate sob of the Christian heart, "I want to know Christ and the power of his resurrection and the fellowship of sharing in his sufferings, becoming like him in his death, and so, somehow, to attain to the resurrection from the dead" (Phil. 3:10-11).

We have spent a lifetime together now, Erling and I, but still there's so much we don't know about each other.

What causes us to react in such unexpected ways to each other at times? Why are we still surprised when we discover that the other one is thinking thoughts that we've never heard her or him express before? Why do we still have a sense sometimes that we really don't know the other one at all? We long to explore all of those inner recesses of each other's mind and spirit, but we don't know the words that will call them forth.

Yet even our longing to know our "beloved" fades before our thirst to understand the mind of Christ. Those who heard him speak reported that they were amazed because he spoke with such authority (Mark 1:27). All we can do is stand amazed, our eyes glued on him, waiting for his next word, his next act. Like the disciples, we follow him, hanging on his every word.

Before this love had come into her life, Sarah had often been lonely. To find a love gives the promise that we will not be lonely again. We reason, rightly, that if someone loves me, that gives me permission to share, to be intimate in my revelations, to share my innermost feelings. Love can fill up the lonely spaces in my life.

Sarah and her beloved have so much to look forward to. They will experience the oneness, the shared secrets, the personal stories, the little laughters, the eye messages. Even if they can never totally enter the self of the other (locked in our human prisons of self as we are), they will come, if they work at it, as close as is humanly possible to knowing another person.

The goal and fulfillment of the Christian's relationship with Jesus is to be "in Christ," wrote Paul. He used that phrase 168 times in his letters. The meaning of the phrase for Paul lay in his appropriation of Christ's identity through Paul's death with Christ on the cross.

> I have been crucified with Christ and I no longer live, but Christ lives in me. The life I live in the body, I live by faith in the Son of God, who loved me and gave himself for me (Gal. 2:20).

Our human love, precious as it is, will always leave us hungering for more. Even the satisfaction of sexual intimacy, fulfilling as it is, lasts but a short time and then the lovers are longing for each other again. And some day Sarah and her beloved will experience the pain and loss and empty loneliness once more when one of them dies and leaves the other alone.

We remember Brian, the young friend from Erling's home town. Brian married Pauline. They both knew when they became engaged that she had primary pulmonary hypertension. A disease of unknown origin, it slowly destroys the arteries in the lungs and ultimately causes heart failure. The eleventh year of their marriage became excruciatingly painful for her, culminating in four heart attacks that finally took her life.

Her last communication with Brian was "I love you," signed with finger pointing to her heart and then to him.

His answer to her was, "I love you with all my heart! Always will, always!"

Human love, with all of its shortcomings and unfulfilled promises, is a mystical sign of what life "in Christ" is like.

But Pauline, being human, had to die. Brian was left alone. Because Brian and Pauline were "in Christ" he was not left comfortless, abandoned, and friendless when she went home to her Creator.

Jesus died but promised his disciples that he would not leave them orphaned (John 14:18), but would send his Holy Spirit, the Comforter, to them.

Now Sarah is "in love." That love will ease the hungry wanting and fill some of the emptiness within her spirit, as love has always done for human lovers everywhere, and it will make more real to both the love of Jesus Christ.

Sarah knows that the kind of love she wants is the love which has its roots in the love of God: "We love because [God] first loved us" (1 John 4:19).

No human love can emulate cross love, God incarnate dying for sinful human beings. Our human loves can simply give us flashing glimpses of that love and help us model it for each other.

To experience all that this means one must accept the love of Christ offered on the cross. Saul spent many years fighting that love. His rejection of Jesus as the promised Messiah of his people led him into violence and bloodshed. In the dramatic confrontation on the Damascus way, Jesus stopped Saul and changed his life forever.

What destructive actions against yourself or others are you engaged in? What emptiness haunts your spirit? What experience of lovelessness still darkens your memories and makes you lash out against others?

Jesus offers you his love. The cross of history stands as an eloquent invitation to you. Its message remains the same, "Come to me."

Why not give the Lord a chance in your life? Why not let the immeasurable riches of God's grace enfold you? The God of the Bible comes running to you with outstretched arms. No one offers greater love, and it's all yours for the taking.

Sit still for a moment. Read again these words from Saul/Paul, converted persecutor, angry man turned lover:

> But because of his great love for us, God, who is rich in mercy, made us alive with Christ even when we were dead in transgressions—it is by grace you have been saved. And God raised us up with Christ and seated us with him in the heavenly realms in Christ Jesus, in order that in the coming ages he might show the incomparable riches of his grace, expressed in his kindness to us in Christ Jesus.
>
> (Eph. 2:4-7)

What more do you want? What are you waiting for? Say yes to Jesus.

Fall in love.

Five

FORGIVENESS, the GIFT of LOVE

As she was coming home one night from her swing-shift job in the post office, Lydia, a grandmother and a widow, was beaten over the head with a piece of pipe and killed.

The Lydia we knew was one of those unique women who leave one blessed after every contact with them. She had once been a Bible teacher in a women's prison and was teaching a class in our church at the time of her death.

Her killer was picked up by the police when he tried to trade her watch for some groceries. Nineteen years of age, he had a history of crime and was labeled as hopelessly incorrigible. His name was Richard Gamble, but because his face was disfigured by a knife scar and one of his eyes was gone, he had earned the name of "One-eyed Gooch."

After his arrest, Lydia's daughter, who was a member of our church, asked for prayers for her mother's killer. "I know that my mother is with the Lord," her daughter said, "and I know that she would want her death to count for Christ. If she were here, she'd say that what she wanted more than anything else was to see her murderer saved. She would want us to pray for him and to try to forgive him."

While they agreed to pray, some of the church members felt that this was a meaningless exercise. How could anyone with Richard's record be "saved"? How could he even be approached?

Richard's trial was held in another city because of threats of lynching. He was found guilty of first-degree murder and sentenced to be executed.

Thinking of his sentence, I (Erling) was struck by the finality of the road ahead for Richard, his last journey. My heart was already heavy. Two other shattering events had taken place in our congregation's life that same summer, the suicide of a mother and the auto-accident death of a young bride. I thought of all the pain that cries out to the heart of God for healing and forgiveness. Now I wanted to go and see Richard. In fact, I felt that I *had* to go.

An appointment was made for me to visit him one Friday at nine o'clock in the morning. I was told that I could speak with him at the county jail before his final transfer to the state penitentiary at Huntsville.

The jail stood stark and naked in the glaring summer sunlight of Texas, barren, cold, aloof. It was so familiar to all of us in the city—the sealed door, high walls, barred windows. I was questioned and searched before the interrogator gave me permission to go in.

I felt a frightening seriousness to my call, but I was uncertain as to what I could say or do.

There was no question about his guilt. As always, sin committed against one person affects so many more. I knew how the brutality and horror of Lydia's death had shattered her family, and I shared the pain of a congregation that had lost a warm Christian friend. I had also caught the fear and hurt of many in the community who were visibly shaken by this meaningless and cruel act.

These thoughts followed me as I was led by a guard deep into the heart of the prison to Richard's cell. I can never forget the hard steel clang as each of the sequence of eight solid doors locked shut behind us.

In the rows of cells, eyes stared at us, blankly or angrily or expectantly or wonderingly. Dark barrenness. Steel bars. Cots. Stench. A shivering dankness. Finally, Richard's cell. The door swung open and shut soundly behind me.

In the semidark there was a moment when I could see nothing. I thought I felt his alienation, his aloneness, his being unwanted. I knew that Richard's life to this point had been one that was empty of love. Born to a couple that broke up soon after his birth, he had drifted unwanted most of his childhood, a product of the lovelessness of so many humans. He grew up clawing and scratching his way, trying to catch a handhold in the fabric of society, struggling against negative odds just to survive.

But Richard didn't make it.

He had scarcely been given any kind of an education. After the knifing that left him scarred, his facial deformity frightened people. He was defeated before he started. No one around him ever hugged him, held him, helped him, or hosted him. Crushed, empty, he learned to struggle and to use his world as he himself had felt used. All of his efforts went for survival in a hostile environment. He had to make it on his own, his feelings warped by the thought of retaliation.

"I'll get even," was the working principle of existence for him. "Somebody'll pay. I don't care who."

Lydia had paid. She was society's sacrifice.

My eyes, adjusted to the darkness of the cell, saw Richard. This was the place of no exit. Hell. What could I say to one who was already there?

I remember being aware of two profound realities. Richard had sinned. He had missed God's mark; he had failed. He knew that, and so did I. But I also knew the Bible's verdict, "All have sinned and fall short of the glory of God" (Rom. 3:23). I, too, was a prisoner in that same cell with the locked door. And "the wages of sin is death." For both of us.

Thank God, another reality confronted us, by far the deepest truth of all: because of Jesus, "the gift of God is eternal life in Christ Jesus our Lord" (Rom. 6:23).

Nothing in the New Testament unveils the depth of this free gift more clearly than an event described in the Gospel of Luke. He wrote that there was a criminal whom tradition has named Dismas hanging high on his cross next to Jesus. This thief had been condemned by society, just as Richard had. He, too, had raged against the uncaring society in which he lived, and he, too, had used people for his own good.

But society had won. It had demanded its "eye for eye" and "tooth for tooth" (Matt. 5:38). Utterly alone, hated, vilified by the crowd, the thief was aware that this was, for him, the end of the way.

Strapped to those crossbars of wood, he was stripped of everything but his voice. Completely aware of the horror of what was happening to him, he heard the one called Jesus telling their executioners, "Father, forgive them; for they do not know what they are doing" (Luke 23:33).

There was something about Jesus' ability to forgive those he should be hating that broke the heart of Dismas. Did Dismas sense another world where a different order reigned, a world where sinners could be forgiven and criminals accepted? The words of Jesus offered him another option. Time was limited. The crushing weight of his own body was rapidly snuffing out his life.

He had no language but a cry, and it echoed in a final forget-me-not over the abyss yawning before him. With the last bit of breath in his collapsing lungs, he cried out over the noises swirling upwards from the crowd below, "Jesus, remember me when you come into your kingdom." Remember me. Let me be one of the forgiven.

Jesus heard. Was there enough strength left in his body for him to lift his head, look over his shoulder and face the dying criminal? Was Dismas looking at him? Did their eyes meet? The answer came. "I tell you the truth, today you will be with me in paradise."

Nothing was more applicable to Richard, it seemed to me, than that statement of Jesus to the lonely one dying beside him.

In that small cell I was face to face with Lydia's murderer. I looked at him. I was prepared by the newspaper account for his disfigured face.

I was keenly aware of myself at that moment. The spotlight appeared to be on me as much as it was on him. I felt my past privileges, my lifetime of good food and of shelter, my education, to be a palpable barrier between us. I felt the need of his forgiveness. In that cell some of my own masks were ripped off, and the realization of my own sinfulness gripped me.

A whole new insight into my own sin swept across my spirit. My world, my society of "respectable" people, calls those things sins that we fancy we don't do, and we elevate those to prominence. We spend a great deal of energy describing and defining "real" sinners who are, of course, the people who do "those" sins. That prevents our secret sins from being unveiled. We are not exposed.

In Richard's cell and in his presence those illusions were shattered. God's list of sinners includes me. Us.

According to Matthew 25, where Jesus unveils the awesome panorama of the end time, it will be not so much what we *did* but what we *did not* that has God's attention.

I who had prided myself on knowing the difference between the law and the gospel, a preacher of the pure "grace" of God in Christ, heard in that cell the words of James and knew that they also were truth:

> What good is it, my brothers, if a man claims to have faith but has no deeds? Can such faith save him? Suppose a brother or sister is without clothes and daily food. If one of you says to him, "Go, I wish you well; keep warm and well fed," but does nothing about his physical needs, what good is it? In the same way, faith by itself, if it is not accompanied by action, is dead.   (James 2:14-17)

I was part of the society that had brought him to this place. The disfigurement of his spirit was done by my world. He was a product of the economic policies that benefited people like me. In that cell I felt as guilty as he. If, as the Scripture says, all have sinned and come short of the glory of God, each of us is in part responsible for the guilt of everyone else.

My mission, at that moment, seemed highly ridiculous. But I was there, and I had come for the purpose of sharing with him what I perceived as the "good news" that Lydia's daughter loved him and wanted him to know of her forgiveness.

So I began, rather hesitantly but picking up speed as I went along. "Richard, the daughter of the woman you murdered sent me to tell you that she loves you and forgives you for killing her mother. The congregation of which I'm the pastor has caught the daughter's love. They want me to tell you that because of Jesus' forgiveness of them, they forgive you, too. They want more than anything else for you to know that same love of Jesus who forgives all of us our sins."

My words came off sounding more sermonic than I had intended.

I waited. Richard mumbled something. He looked at me. I felt so patronizing, so smug. But I went on pleading with him to accept the offered love and forgiveness of Jesus. I spent 20 minutes more with him. He thanked me and I left.

I did not feel very successful in my "mission."

Soon after, Richard was taken to Huntsville to wait for his execution.

That's where the impossible happened. Somehow a Bible reached him from another inmate. A well-known verse in the Gospel of John had been marked for his attention:

For God so loved the world that he gave his one and only Son, that whoever believes in him shall not perish but have eternal life (John 3:16).

In that promise Richard's Savior spoke to him and possessed him. Even behind his prison bars Richard was set free.

Before he went to his death a few weeks later, he told another prisoner on death row about the good news he had experienced. Richard brought that prisoner to the same forgiving love.

The largest daily newspaper in Fort Worth reported on its front page that Richard Gamble, singing hymns, went to his death.

"Truly I say to you, Richard, today you will be with me in paradise."

Richard had received the most loving gift anyone can give or receive, the gift of forgiveness, both from God and from his fellow human beings.

Forgiveness is the ultimate gift of love. To be able to say, "I love you and forgive you," to someone who has utterly wronged you is the visible expression of the glory of God.

Our age knows only too well that the natural response when we have been wronged is to retaliate with vengeance. We struggle to match injury to injury, violence to violence, hatred to hatred.

Our daily news is filled with this response. The tragedy of retaliation is that it breeds more retaliation. If one neighbor is thinking only of how to get even with another neighbor, then we live in a sealed-off world.

Mary was a widow in our town. When part of her fence fell into her neighbor's yard, breaking some of their bushes, they retaliated by knocking her whole fence down one night and scattering the pieces in her yard before she could do anything about the mishap.

Out of Richard Gamble's pain and anger, he had retaliated against the society he saw as the cause of his condition. Society had retaliated by demanding his condemnation and death.

When I walked out of the prison that day into the summer sun of Texas, and the last of the doors shut behind me, I appreciated my freedom in Christ in a way I had never known it before.

Back in his cell I had stood condemned with Richard. Hadn't Jesus said, "You have heard that it was said to the people long ago, 'Do not murder, and anyone who murders will be subject to judgment.'" That was a word for Richard, the murderer.

But the word goes on. "But I tell you that anyone who is angry with his brother will be subject to judgment. Again, anyone who says to his brother, 'Raca,' is answerable to the Sanhedrin. But anyone who says, 'You fool!' will be in danger of the fire of hell" (Matt. 5:21-22). That's the word for Erling, the pastor.

Jesus sees the heart. Although I was not given to outbursts of anger (anger was not an acceptable response in my boyhood home), I could be very sarcastic under the veil of humor. And I knew that in thoughtlessness or fun I had sometimes called people "idiots"! If Richard's cell was hell, Erling deserved to be there with him.

So when I stood outside the prison, a free man, I knew what it meant to be forgiven, no longer under the penalty of death. Richard had to pay for his crimes against society, but the love of God had already paid for his and my sins on the cross.

Eternal life lay beyond death for both of us.

Forgiveness is God's greatest gift.

The final book of the Bible, Revelation, is alive with hymns that cannot be contained or controlled. The heavenly doxologies of the redeemed peal across the expanse of the cosmos. All of those who have accepted the Lamb's forgiveness are radiant with the glory of the "Lamb, who was slain," whose blood ransomed us for God "from every tribe and language and people and nation" (Rev. 5:12,9)!

But forgiveness is not just a key to get us to heaven.

Forgiveness is the heart of love and the key to loving relationships. How many times we have wished we could take a feuding husband and wife and force them to say to each other "I'm sorry, forgive me," and have the other one respond with "Of course, I forgive you."

But that's too easy, isn't it?

Instead we seem to find it necessary to keep a list of wrongs done to us by the other one, lists that reach far into the past and dredge up from the cobwebbed corridors of time all the sins committed against our love.

We continue to pray, "Forgive us our sins, as we forgive those who sin against us," but in reality we wait, withholding our forgiveness, hardening our self-righteous hearts in the conviction that some people don't deserve to be forgiven. What they have done is too bad.

Did Richard Gamble deserve to be forgiven, to go to his death singing hymns of joy in Jesus?

Do Erling and Marge Wold deserve to be forgiven?

Do you deserve to be forgiven?

By focusing this chapter on the very obvious crime of Richard Gamble, we may be diverting attention from the daily need for repentance and forgiveness. Relationships are built on our being able to say, "I'm sorry," and to forgive one another in the context of daily life.

The often-heard statement, "I can forgive, but I can never forget," does not echo God's policy!

In the Bible the word "forgiveness" has the meaning of "send away" or "wipe away." Once sin is forgiven, it's gone! It has been wiped away from the memory of God, sent away into the depths of the sea, obliterated from everyone's sight.

"I can't forget" might be interpreted as "I *won't* forget." Behind those words are a desire for revenge or the wish to make the other person suffer for what she or he has done. We won't make forgiveness as easy as God did! Never!

Repentance is a prerequisite for forgiveness, of course. The first call from Jesus and from his messenger, John the Baptizer, was a call to repentance.

But repentance is not a call to wallow in guilt, though

it pierces us with the sharp pain of regret. Rather it means a commitment to a new course of action. When we forgive, we accept repentance as an authentic statement of the other person's intention to change.

So convinced is Jesus of this that he asks us to forgive each other not only seven times, but seventy times seven! In our lifetimes, how many times do you think God has forgiven each one of us?

Forgiveness is a mirror of love. Theologian Paul Tillich once said that it means reconciliation in spite of estrangement, reunion in spite of hostility, acceptance of those who are unacceptable, and reception of those who are rejected.

Forgiveness always gives us the possibility of starting over again, of beginning something new. The apostle Paul captures this wonder when he writes, "If anyone is in Christ," that person is a new creation. "The old has gone," he says. "The new has come!" (2 Cor. 5:17).

Do you have a relationship that needs newness?

Try forgiveness. Practice forgiving, work at it.

We have used a formula of confession and absolution in our own marriage that we describe in our book, *Bible Readings for Couples*. We hold hands and say the following:

Husband: I confess to you, my wife, that I have sinned against you in these ways . . . (Confess the feelings that have blurred your love. Be honest.) I am sorry and ask your forgiveness because I don't want anything to stand between us.

Wife: I have heard your confession, my husband, and I forgive you in the name of Jesus and out of my own love for you. I, too, want to confess that I have sinned against you in the following ways . . . (Make honest confession of the feelings that have blurred your love.) I am sorry and ask your forgiveness because I don't want anything to stand between us.

Husband: I have heard your honest confession, and I forgive you in the name of Jesus and out of my own love for you.

Of course, it's necessary to repeat the above frequently, because the very fact of living and loving requires daily confessing and forgiving.

When you forgive another, you give your very life to that other person. In your forgiving, you are saying to him or her, "I'm making myself open to you, vulnerable, knowing that I may be hurt again."

In our vulnerability we imitate Jesus, who captures the essence of God's forgiveness in the words, "This is my blood . . . poured out for many for the forgiveness of sins" (Matt. 26:28). Whenever we accept God's forgiveness in Holy Communion, we share in Christ's body and blood.

> Is not the cup of thanksgiving for which we give thanks a participation in the blood of Christ? And is not the bread that we break a participation in the body of Christ? Because there is one loaf, we, who are many, are one body, for we all partake of the one loaf. (1 Cor. 10:16-17)

When we forgive those who sin against us, we are participating in the very person and death of Christ.

As we practice forgiving, we come to understand the holy mystery of the Eucharist. God has heard our cry, "For God's sake, love me!" and gives us what we need—forgiveness.

Jesus tied forgiveness and the "altar" together when he told the disciples:

> Therefore, if you are offering your gift at the altar and there remember that your brother has something against you, leave your gift there in front of the altar. First go and be reconciled to your brother [or sister]; then come and offer your gift. (Matt. 5:23-24)

When we explore all that forgiveness means, we lack the language to express the unfolding layers of grace upon grace. All we can do is to stand under the cross and accept the gracious words, "Father, forgive them," and to accept our assignment, by the grace of God, to practice forgiving.

Lydia, the murdered one, and Richard, her murderer, stand in the presence of God through the same miracle of forgiving love.

Lord, forgive us our sins as we forgive those who sin against us.

Lord, remember me when you come into your kingdom.

Lord, remember Lydia.

Remember Richard.

Remember me.

Six

THE RESPONSE to LOVE

We were at a dinner party. The hostess insisted that we not sit with our friends or our spouses but next to someone we had never met before.

I (Marge) was seated next to a man in his mid-30s and immediately experienced a frantic internal quest for some topic of conversation that would cross the barrier of unfamiliarity. We exchanged names.

"I'm Phil," he said and then asked what I was involved in. I told him about my work with congregations in changing communities. He expressed polite interest and then proceeded to tell me about himself. He owned his own business, he said, one that made a lot of money and enabled him to own an expensive home, a second house, and a yacht. He had it all, but it had not brought him any great sense of fulfillment or accomplishment.

"I had it all," he said, "but I kept feeling that there was something I had left undone, that before I died there was something else I was supposed to do with my education and my skills, in fact, with my life."

One night as he was watching the evening news, his wandering, halfhearted attention was caught by a picture of Southeast Asian "boat people" as they drifted helplessly in the ocean seeking a friendly port to receive them. They had been sent out of their own country and were unacceptable additions to the swollen post-Vietnam war populations of other countries in the area. At that point in the news program a reporter came into the picture to announce that Thailand had offered to permit the boats full of sick and hungry people to land in that country, but they had no place to house the thousands who were accepting the invitation.

"That night," my dinner partner said, "I called my travel agent and told her to get me two tickets on the next plane for Thailand, one for me and one for my son who was in college. My wife thought I had lost my mind, but I knew it was something I was being called to do."

He and his son went to Thailand and offered their services to various agencies and were finally accepted by a United Nations work group. Their assignment was to mobilize the boat people to build a shelter for ten thousand refugees! They stayed six months.

A radical reordering of all of their priorities literally revolutionized the lives of Phil and his son. A new vision completely altered their life-style.

There at the dinner table, surrounded by the chatter of other guests, I felt transported to another dimension of reality.

The Bible is alive to this possibility. It wants to sweep us up with its encounters with Jesus into another agenda for living.

We catch a glimpse of that in the life of Zacchaeus (Luke 19:1-10). This lonely man, hiding high in a tree, found himself deliberately approached by Jesus, who merely asked him for the privilege of spending some time in Zacchaeus's house. This simple request revolutionized Zacchaeus's life.

Zacchaeus was well aware that he was an outcast, unwanted member of his society, despised by others because of his occupation. He was a tax collector. As the highest bidder, he had bought and won the rights to collect taxes in Palestine for the Roman government, which was the military occupant of that land. As long as Rome got its share, it was his protected privilege to extort as much as he could from every person or event. The extortion money was his salary.

In that brief encounter with Jesus, Zacchaeus discovered a dazzling love. We see him exploding with unbelievable energy released in him like a geyser. The naked love of Jesus affected the center of his existence and sent him running home to arrange for the coming of the Nazarene.

One loving word from Jesus and Zacchaeus's whole life was decisively altered. This man, who had formerly been controlled by greed, blurted out, without hesitation and without coaxing, "I want to give half of all that I have to the poor. If I have taken anything wrongfully from anyone, I'll repay that person four times more."

Dramatic. Unreal. How could a person's outlook on life change so suddenly?

Zacchaeus can be understood only by someone who has had a similar encounter with Jesus. Then Zacchaeus's behavior is seen as the "normal" reaction to the new world of the kingdom of God as Jesus revealed it.

Zacchaeus saw in the behavior of Jesus an infinite compassion for people, people like himself, that he had never seen before. He saw himself, no longer despised, but worthy. He saw himself made in the image of God. He saw how he had been using others who were made in the image of God.

They were more valuable than all of the things he had been collecting.

Concern for others is not paramount in the mind-set of our present western society. Getting rich is the "in" thing. Telecasts about the rich and famous, the unscrupulous power people, fascinate us. College and university students talk openly about using their education as a means for getting rich. They, too, want to "have it all."

Some of this longing may be born out of a basic, gut-deep insecurity. Analysts repeatedly say that young people are running scared. Systems change so rapidly that sources of security can easily be destroyed.

Part of this hunger simply roots itself deeply in the worship of two hoary old idols: power and profit. Buying may be the god of our country and our age. We are enslaved to acquiring. The media in all of its forms supports this "religion." Greed is glorified; money is deified. Control is its objective.

Yet dreams that find their fulfillment in acquiring things often fail to realize their promise. A study done by Northwestern University found that the newly rich, state lottery winners, said that they were happier with what they had acquired, but that their everyday activities were actually less pleasurable. The high point of winning the lottery made ordinary pleasures pale by comparison. "If we seek life-satisfactions through material achievements," the study said, "we will need a continually expanded level of affluence to maintain the old level of contentment."

Phil, my dinner partner, discovered that truth in his own life. He broke out of the imprisoning syndrome described by one wealthy person who, when asked, "How much is enough?" simply answered, "More." Such an insatiable obsession can destroy the very significance of being human.

If I struggle only for *my* good, *my* advantage, *my* profit, I become sealed in my own tomb. I lose my world. I become a living mummy struggling to use the world to promote my own cause.

That point of view was flippantly articulated when someone said, "The robber on the cross did nothing for anyone, but he was saved."

A friend replied, "He is a *dead* robber. You are a living one."

If one is lost in a search for things to fill one's emptiness, that search becomes all-consuming. One misses the opportunity to discover and explore the whole world.

Phil was like that. Sitting in front of his television set that night, watching the news, he heard the call to love and saw himself sitting there watching a picture of incredibly agonizing need while the reality behind the picture was leaving him unmoved!

Half dozing in his chair, Phil experienced a moment of startled awakedness.

What's the matter with me? he thought. *I'm sitting here watching these people being tossed by the waves, dying in an overcrowded little boat, nobody wanting them to come into their safe harbors, and I'm acting as if this was a movie with make-believe characters who will soon go home to their families and dinners when the day's filming is over!*

In that moment of insight Phil became fully human. In a profound sense he also became totally divine. He saw life through the eyes of Jesus. That vision was like a tremendous jolt of lightning, killing forever the person he used to be and energizing him to become the person he was meant to be. Phil began to live.

An associate of that remarkable legendary doctor Tom Dooley who literally gave his life to the poor in Asia, told us what Tom Dooley said just before he died. "I could have been a doctor for the rich in New York," he said, "and have become rich and internationally famous myself. But my heart kept repeating, 'Give your life to the poor, give your life to the poor.' I followed my heart."

More than 20 years ago God made Tom Dooley world famous. He received more in giving than in taking.

We are called to have God live in us. Jesus wants to move about within and through our bodies. Doesn't Paul say he agonized "until Christ is formed in you" (Gal. 4:19)?

Phil and Zacchaeus, gripped by a compelling Christ, had to find a channel of expression for their new understanding of who they were. No longer could they see themselves simply as Phil, the certified public accountant, or Zacchaeus, the tax collector, but they were disciples of the One who had given his life for the life of the world.

What did Jesus talk about to Zacchaeus when he came to his house?

Maybe he talked about the politics of oppression and control. Zacchaeus supported an oppressive government whose exorbitant demands on the economy of the country crushed the poor of the land. Jesus always evidenced a burning compassion for the ill-used, the degraded, the abused, the "little people." He spoke his troubling words of rebuke, "Woe is you!" to cities like Korazin and Bethsaida (Matt. 11:21) because of their lack of repentance.

Then again Jesus may have talked to Zacchaeus about his mother Mary and her politics. Why not? Mary's influence on Jesus must have been enormous. Luke, the gospel writer, gave her credit for some startling lyrics. She sang a song about the kind of God who sent her the word about the son that was to be born to her.

He has scattered those who are proud in their inmost
   thoughts.

He has brought down rulers from their thrones,
   but has lifted up the humble.
He has filled the hungry with good things,
   but has sent the rich away empty.

(Luke 1:51-53)

In her hymn of exaltation Mary saw the totality of God's power directed toward the care of the poor. God scatters, God brings down, God fills. Her vision is one of God's work in this world, reshaping it, making everything conform to God's will for the oppressed.

Perhaps Jesus went on to tell Zacchaeus about his own first sermon in his home town of Nazareth. When he came back to the synagogue where he had grown up, he gathered there with his fellow townspeople and was given the Scripture to read. He opened it to Isaiah and read:

The Spirit of the Lord is on me, because
   he has anointed me to preach good news to the poor.
He has sent me to proclaim freedom for the prisoners
   and recovery of sight for the blind,
     to release the oppressed.

(Luke 4:18)

Jesus was not only a true son of Mary, but he was the true Son of God. His "theology" and his "program" were directly out of the heart of God and the words of Scripture.

Above all Jesus knew that his task as the Messiah, God's anointed one, was to usher in the kingdom, or the reign, of God. It was the description of that reign that he read in Nazareth.

God's reign is that order in which the values of the world are turned upside down. It's the people at the bottom of the world's economic pyramids who are of prime concern to God. God's justice does not support a "royal" religion whose aim is to please the wealthy, the powerful, the privileged. God's kingdom, ushered in by the Messiah, is destined to upset that established worldly order.

When we read about the abysmal poverty that afflicts the lives of one-third of the 320 million Latin Americans, just one fraction of the world's poor, we sense the pain that burdens the heart of God. The poor in that continent earn less per family in one year than the average American family spends on food for one week.

The cause? Always, as in every country where massive poverty exists, the cause is a manipulation of the economic system by those in power who use the poor for their own profit.

If the church of Jesus Christ is to model what the reign of God is like, it must capture the compassion of all of its people.

In Latin America 1500 priests, nuns, friars, bishops, and lay people have been arrested or kidnaped, questioned, tortured, exiled, or assassinated in the decade from 1968-78, because they've taken the risk of providing options for the poor.

The church of Jesus Christ has the freedom to speak out for the oppressed, the powerless, and the poor. The words are so clearly written in the Scripture:

> If there is a poor man among your brothers in any of the towns of the land that the Lord your God is giving you, do not be hardhearted or tightfisted toward your poor brother. Rather be openhanded and freely lend him whatever he needs. . . . Give generously to him and do so without a grudging heart; then because of this the Lord your God will bless you in all your work and in everything you put your hand to. There will always be poor people in the land. Therefore I command you to be openhanded toward your brothers and toward the poor and needy in your land.
>
> (Deut. 15:7-8,10-11)

God, the Father of Jesus, is a just God who hears the cry of the migrant, of the widow and the orphan, and of the poor. For God, the scales of justice are always tipped in favor of the poor and the oppressed.

God's Messiah, the prophet Isaiah had said, would judge the needy with righteousness, and "with justice he will give decisions for the poor of the earth" (Isa. 11:4), as he ushered in the kingdom of God.

Like the God from whom he came, Jesus the Messiah would be a "refuge for the poor, a refuge for the needy in his distress, a shelter from the storm and a shade from the heat" (Isa. 25:4).

Zacchaeus knew instantly that his commitment to give half of his earnings to the poor would please Jesus. The sin of Zacchaeus was simply that he had oppressed and robbed the poor in order to become rich himself.

Phil, sitting in front of his television set watching the poor people in their overcrowded boats being sent from one country to another, saw in them the face of Jesus, who said of himself that "Foxes have holes and birds of the air have nests, but the Son of Man has no place to lay his head" (Matt. 8:20). Like Zacchaeus, Phil had to respond to what he saw.

Jesus said that whatever we do for those who have a need is really done for him (Matt. 25:40). When the kingdom is finally realized and the Son of Man returns in his final glory, only those will inherit his kingdom who have fed the hungry, clothed the naked, visited the sick, and come to those in prison.

Before him, on the television screen, Phil saw them all—the hungry, the naked, the sick, the captives, the homeless. When his vision saw through their "disguises" and revealed the Christ in their suffering, the love of Christ compelled him to do something about what he saw. "For Christ's love compels us. . ." (2 Cor. 5:14).

Phil responded in faith, not knowing what he was to do but simply knowing that he had to respond. Intuitively he seemed to understand what the founder of the Vincent de Paul Society (a Catholic organization that ministers to the poor in the world) learned. This remarkable French priest of the 17th century said to his followers before he died, "It is only by your love that the poor will forgive you for your loaf of bread and your bowl of soup."

Phil, with his two homes, all the food he needed through all of his lifetime, money in the bank and cash in his pocket, left it all to share in the life of the Christ he saw in the faces of the boat people that day.

Phil experienced exactly what is happening to so many of his age group, the so-called "yuppie generation." These young urban professionals, careerists who are struggling to "have it all in a have-not world" and who have been remarkably successful in achieving their goals, are now reported to be plagued by feelings of profound spiritual emptiness. They have found, said a recent broadcaster, that far too often their work is controlling but unrewarding. Their hearts say they must find fulfillment, idealism, and possibilities for relationships.

Phil found his rewarding relationships among the boat people. In the six months during which he worked with them, built shelters with them, ate the food they ate, shared their lives, he learned what love can be and do.

The love he gave was returned so powerfully and in such rich measure that it changed his life. He knew, experientially, that "The kingdom of God is not a matter of eating and drinking, but of righteousness, peace and joy in the Holy Spirit" (Rom. 14:17). Like that tax collector of old, Phil discovered that God's love is not to be hoarded but to be given away to others. That's what brings peace and joy.

If "for God's sake, love me!" is the cry of the world's people, then how will that cry be answered except through us, the people who have received the love of God?

When last we heard of him, Phil had sold his business and uses the income to sail from country to country in his yacht, bringing his own personal aid and whatever he can collect from friends and business associates. Dropping anchor wherever there is a need, he lives among the people with his family, loves them, and helps in any way he can to address their need. Exuberantly, he gives away what he never knew he possessed before and is enriched many times more than he had ever been in his previous life.

In the *Christian Science Monitor* (December 1, 1975), a French missionary, Pierre Pradervand, described this enrichment, writing about his new homeland, Africa.

Oh, the gentleness of black Africa, the light, the human warmth, the embrace of the heart meet one everywhere. Always the children run up to you, trusting, joyful. If there is one word above all I would use to describe this part of Africa, it would be gentleness.

What is civilization? If there is any one place in the world I have met a "civilization of the heart" it is in rural Africa. . . .

If our hearts are old, or tired, or cynical, or self-satisfied, thus shall we see the world. But if we are still, and let the youthful expectation of love and goodness fill our hearts, we will see goodness and love all around us. They are there, waiting to be seen. . . . As I listen with ears of the soul and look with the eyes of the heart, much beauty unfolds, many "dark areas" glow with the brightest light, many "foreign" people whose language I do not understand become friends.

If the world is crying "for God's sake, love me!" from every corner of our globe, it may be possible that we, those of us who are the body of Christ in this world, are the answer, God's answer, to that cry.

Seven

LOVE AND
the SUFFERER

I was totally unprepared for Sally. She was one of my hospice patients, and she knew that she was considered "terminal." No one is accepted for hospice unless they have been pronounced beyond hope of a medical cure.

I had come to expect that my patients would be emaciated, probably comatose, heavily medicated, and in much pain. My previous patient had been in that condition all of the six weeks I knew her before her death.

When the hospice volunteer coordinator called to tell me that Sally was my new patient, she said, "Sally will probably die within a month and certainly by Christmas." It was then the week before Thanksgiving.

She went on to describe Sally's condition. "Sally is 35 years old and has cancer of the cervix. The cancer caused a bowel obstruction, so she has a colostomy. She also has a nephrostomy since her kidneys stopped working for a while last summer and her bladder also had to be removed. She's alone with her 15-year-old son from a previous marriage. She'd been married to her present husband for only a year when she got sick, and he left her. No one knows where he is now."

I called the number she gave me and got directions to the apartment from the boy who answered, evidently Sally's son.

I walked through the maze of apartments looking for the building with Sally's number on it and rehearsed my opening remarks. I would be serious, I thought, but not too serious. I would not stay more than 15 minutes so that I wouldn't wear her out. I would be friendly but not familiar so as not to intrude on her privacy.

I was also concerned about the difference in our ages. *Wouldn't she prefer a younger volunteer?* I wondered. First visits were always hard for me.

The apartment with her number on it was in a dark back corner on the first floor of the building. There was no window or light, and in the dark I wasn't sure the door had the right number, so I felt the raised letters with my fingers like a blind person reading Braille. I lifted the knocker and hit the door a tentative knock.

"Come on in," a young, musical voice called out.

I pushed the door open and stepped into a small, crowded living room. A sofa, a chair, a coffee table, a television set, a VCR, and a desk had been pushed aside to make room for a Christmas tree. A bird swooped down from somewhere and landed on my shoulder, where she proceeded to peck at my earring.

"Leave Marge alone, Tasha, and come here," said a very pretty young woman sitting on a single-sized wooden bed against the wall. She was fully clothed in jeans and a bright blue blouse. "I'm Sally, and of course you're Marge," she said. "Are you hungry? Help yourself to pop. It's in the refrigerator, and there are some cookies around that my nurse brought. My goodness, but you're pretty! Peggy told me how old you were, but I'd never believe it."

That was the beginning of my relationship with Sally. My carefully rehearsed plans for the visit were never used.

I stayed an hour and a half that first day and learned all about Sally. Everything the coordinator had told me was true, except that she had not told me how beautiful Sally was. Big, black, heavy-lashed eyes looked out of a delicately featured face. Long black hair hung down to her waist.

"Didn't you have chemotherapy?" I asked.

"It made my hair thin," Sally explained.

I wondered how thick it had been before. As I said, I was totally unprepared for Sally.

I was with her for nine months. She did not die before Christmas; she lived until the next August.

Suffering is endemic in the human race, and we all share in it. We have known suffering and you probably have, too. Even so, it was difficult for me to comprehend the lifetime of suffering which had been Sally's lot. Her history included abusive parents, a stepfather who raped her and her two sisters, forcing her to run away from home in her early teens. From that time on, her life consisted of a series of men who took her in, cast her out, married her, and divorced her. Somehow she managed to get a cosmetology license and a business-college education.

Her cancer was misdiagnosed as a cervical "infection" and remained untreated for two years until she wondered why she kept on hemorrhaging and went to another doctor. By that time it was too late. The cancer had metastasized into other organs. The only bitter words I ever heard Sally speak were reserved for the doctor who had diagnosed her wrongly, because no one needs to die of cervical cancer if it is promptly treated.

How can life be so bad for some people? What did I

do to deserve being born into a loving family with a father who worked every day he could at some job or another to keep us all in food and shelter, who never abused, neglected, or abandoned us? Why was I so fortunate as to have a mother who was always jolly and who found in her home and her family enough satisfaction for a lifetime?

Of course, those questions are beyond my answering. The sufferings of Job never did get answered to anyone's satisfaction in the great story of his experience in the Old Testament. Do you remember that story? The man Job was "blameless and upright; he feared God and shunned evil," says the Bible. He was "the greatest man among all the people of the East" with a wife, children, herds of animals, many servants (Job 1:1-3).

But one day God granted the request of Satan to take away all of Job's wealth and children when Satan insisted that the only reason Job loved and served God was because he had never been given the opportunity to curse God. When permission was given to Satan by God to test Job, immediately some enemies came and killed his animals and servants, a fire from heaven consumed others, and a great wind blew down his house and killed all of his children!

What was Job's reaction to all of this tragedy? "Naked I came from my mother's womb, and naked I will depart. The Lord gave and the Lord has taken away; may the name of the Lord be praised" (Job 1:21).

Since this was not the response Satan desired, he went to God again. When God pointed out to him that Job still loved God even after all of his losses, Satan had an answer ready: "Skin for skin! A man will give all he has for his own life. But stretch out your hand and strike his flesh and bones, and he will surely curse you to your face" (2:4-5).

Again God gave Satan permission to do whatever he wanted with Job, except he had to spare Job's life.

In the next scene Job, afflicted with "painful sores from the soles of his feet to the top of his head," sits among the ashes and scrapes himself with a broken piece of pottery and his suffering was great.

His friends came to commiserate with him.

Job cried out to them, "Why was I ever conceived? Why was I born? Why didn't I die at birth? Why did I ever see the light?"

He complained about God's treatment of him. "God has worn me out," he cried.

Yet through all of his pain and despair he never cursed God. Even his wife thought that was being rather foolish, and she urged him to "Curse God and die!" (2:9).

His three friends—Eliphaz, Bildad, and Zophar—piously mouthed all of the traditional reasons for suffering: Job had sinned and was being punished; he was a hypocrite and needed to repent; God is sovereign and would reward Job if he would only stop lying to God. Job was haughty and obstinate, they insisted, and he kept on sinning by accusing God of being unjust in his punishment of Job's sins.

When they finished their boring and accusatory speeches and Job still insisted that he didn't deserve all the loss and pain he was suffering, a younger man named Elihu came and berated Job for justifying himself and for not recognizing that God had the right to discipline and chasten Job. Job's suffering, said Elihu, was to accomplish Job's sanctification. (Aren't these the reasons you've been given for your suffering or that you've given to others when they've suffered?)

Finally, God appeared in person to Job and pointed out that God's ways are not our ways but in everything they are superior to anything human beings can understand or devise. God, in fact, became very angry with Job's friends for all their pious platitudes. He told them to ask Job to pray for them so they could be forgiven for their self-righteousness, which had angered God.

What was it that Job understood about suffering that his friends did not? Job said to his wordy friends, "I also could speak like you, if you were in my place; I could make fine speeches against you and shake my head at you" (16:4). Talk is cheap when one is not the sufferer, and Job would not accept their pat and pious answers!

Apparently neither will God.

The Book of Job asks the question, "Why do the righteous suffer?" and gives no answer except that God knows about it and is in our sufferings with us. Suffering is not retribution for our wrongdoings, nor is it God's way of disciplining us, according to the Book of Job. One must simply trust that God, who made everything, is still present in our sufferings and still loves us in it and through it all. Suffering is no denial of our cry for love.

Like Job, Sally knew this. She never blamed God for the evil human beings had done to her. For every abuse she had suffered from some people, she insisted that she had received much more in the way of love and compassion from others.

Sally had become a Christian just a year before she died. In July of the year I met her, she was rushed to the hospital with acute kidney failure. The doctors gave her no more than two days to live. A young woman friend who was a Christian came and asked Sally if she could pray for her. Immediately after her prayer, Sally's kidneys started working again. Even with a very meager knowledge of the Christian faith, Sally believed that God had touched her.

When she was accepted for hospice care shortly after that experience, she was assigned a home-care nurse who happened to be a member of our church, a young woman about Sally's age. That nurse knew that I was without a patient at the time, because my previous patient had just died, and she recommended me to be Sally's hospice volunteer.

To Sally, all of this was God's doing. When she learned that my husband was a pastor, she insisted on coming to church with her visiting nurse. All through Lent and Holy Week, she identified with Jesus, God's "suffering servant."

One of the gifts that Sally possessed that Job did not was a manifest joy in living. I was told, you recall, that Sally would die before Christmas. Instead, she went out dancing on New Year's Eve with her nurse and her nurse's fiancé! In March some friends invited her to go to Mexico with them. She lay in the back of their station wagon and came back loaded with inexpensive gifts for everybody. Two weeks before she died, between emergency trips to the hospital because of excessive hemorrhaging, she used her last disability check to rent a white limousine to take her closest friends out for a ride and to dinner!

Sally lived every day as if it were her last chance to love and to be loved.

I wrote some notes when my husband was lying paralyzed in the hospital after his surfing accident. Sitting in the waiting room outside of the intensive care unit, I wrote these words:

> Why do we take such comfort in the words, "This too will pass?" It seems to me that one should enter into every moment, grip it, drain it of all of its meaning and savor all of its sensations. To run away from an experience is to choose sensory sedation. We are here to feel, to explore, to dig into, to know.

Sally savored everything. She loved life in all of its forms. During the months I knew her, she bred, raised, and gave away dozens of pet birds. She had a new puppy and was training him in the months before her death.

Her son was the joy of her life. She wanted to live until he could take care of himself and worked to have him declared an independent minor. Five months before her death she insisted on moving into an apartment with more light, because she thought he would rather live there after she died. In spite of her pain, she packed and carried boxes, and we got her moved and settled. She bought second-hand furniture and knew exactly when and where garage and yard sales were being held.

Sally taught me that the way to handle suffering is not to give in to it and to accept it without fighting. Nor, on the other hand, is it to live in a perpetual state of denial of the seriousness of suffering and of the inevitability of death. Somewhere in between those two states of being is the option of living each day as fully as possible, using everything that medicine and faith can offer to make life as bearable and joyous as it can be.

Time (December 29, 1986) carried an excellent article, "A Letter to the Year 2086," in which Roger Rosenblatt said, "If I have a fatal brain tumor, I know exactly where to go for the best mechanical support. *But who will tell me how to face my death?*" (italics ours). Who indeed?

Death is inevitable for all of us. The hope and longing for a time and a place where pain will be no more, where suffering will have ended and God is all in all, is a groaning in our spirit. Paul's inspired words to the Christians in Rome express the longing so well:

> I consider that our present sufferings are not worth comparing with the glory that will be revealed in us. The creation waits in eager expectation. . . . the creation itself will be liberated from its bondage to decay and brought into the glorious freedom of the children of God. (Rom. 8:18-19, 21)

When that time comes, wrote John in Revelation, God will be with us, and God will wipe away every tear from our eyes. "There will be no more death or mourning or crying or pain, for the old order of things has passed away" (Rev. 21:3-4).

Until that time comes, there remains only you and me to wipe away the tears from the eyes of the suffering and the dying. God is not here yet to do it in person, but must channel love through our persons.

Hospice volunteers are trained to give unconditional love to the dying persons assigned to them. Often family members are afraid of "catching cancer" from the patient, and they may stop touching that person. Hospice volunteers hug patients, hold them, kiss their cheeks hello and good-bye, and demonstrate to the family that the patients need, more than ever, to know that they are accepted and loved— and respected. I never just dropped in on Sally without calling her beforehand and asking her permission to come. Being sick does not make one into a "thing."

We have it in our power to bring life and healing to others through our compassion and love or to destroy them with our lovelessness.

The only time I saw Sally crushed, like a flower trampled under careless feet, was when she came back from a plane trip to Phoenix where she went because she wanted to visit her only cousin and to see his new baby before she (Sally) died. Her son bought her a plane ticket with his earnings as a busboy at an expensive restaurant.

When she was on the plane for her return trip to Los Angeles, the agent came in and asked her to disembark because some of the other passengers had complained about the odor that surrounded her. When Sally explained that she had to get back home that day for one of her treatments, the flight attendants put her in a front seat and moved all

of the other passengers to seats at least two rows behind her.
To make sure that no one would sit near her, they removed
all of the cushions from the seats around her.

To Sally, who bathed herself several times a day,
changed her dressings constantly, used special deodorants
liberally, and sprayed herself with cologne, this treatment
was devastating to her already diminished ego.

So much depends on us. Our attitudes and our actions
either increase the sufferings of others or give them the will
and the ability to endure their suffering. We are part of the
great "cloud of witnesses," which the letter to the Hebrews
describes, that enables others to "run with perseverance the
race marked out for us" (Heb. 12:1). Like the Hebrew Christians we are witnesses to Jesus, pointing to him as "the
author and perfecter of our faith, who for the joy set before
him endured the cross, scorning its shame."

Love is a natural healing medicine we all possess in
inexhaustible supply, and the more of it we give away, the
more we have to share.

Evil, on the other hand, is anything that kills another
person—in mind, body, or spirit. So many people had con-
spired in her lifetime to kill Sally—her parents who had
abused her, all of the men who had used her, the doctor
who treated her for the wrong disease, the people on the
plane who objected to the odor of a dying woman.

In order to counteract the evil that others generated,
the people who loved her had to work all the harder to
produce enough of their love as an antidote to keep her alive.

With Satan working so hard to destroy life, the people
of God who have the Spirit of Jesus are called to give God's
love and life to the world. We are part of the great cosmic
struggle between good and evil that nailed Jesus to the cross
but that also called forth his triumphant resurrection from

the dead. Love rolled away the stone in front of his tomb and destroyed the power of Satan forever.

In the months before her death I had taken Sally regularly to the county medical center for radiation treatments and hospital visits. I knew that she had a fear of dying there alone if she had to go there for her final emergency.

Our prayers were that she could be with caring people when she died. In the middle of her last night she had to call the paramedics herself. When they saw how ill she was, they took her to the hospital nearest to her apartment. That happened to be a Lutheran hospital. It was the only time she ever went there. The chaplain stayed with her from the time she was admitted until her death an hour later. By the time I got there she had already died. Sally, the sufferer, was at rest.

God had answered her prayer. She was not alone in her dying. God's love had seen to that.

> Even though I walk
>   through the valley of the shadow of death,
> I will fear no evil,
>   for you are with me;
>   your rod and your staff,
>   they comfort me.
>
> (Ps. 23:4)

Eight

LOVE AND
the SKEPTIC

One night ten years ago the telephone rang at midnight, waking us from the sound sleep of those early hours of the morning. Our son John's voice, trembling with urgency, came over the wire. "Mom, Dad," he addressed us, "can you come over right away? Something's happening to me, and I need to talk to someone right away."

We dressed quickly, preoccupied with our own questionings and the emotions aroused in us by the obvious distress in John's voice. Neither one of us spoke much during the hour-long drive on the quiet nighttime freeway to the apartment where John and Diane were spending his sabbatical.

John, the oldest of our five children, had always been an excellent student, graduating from college with honors as valedictorian of his class. He had no trouble getting accepted at Johns Hopkins University, one of the top graduate schools in the country in political science, his field of study. When he received his Ph.D., he accepted a teaching position on the faculty of one of the California state universities. Now he was on his first sabbatical leave and involved in some research on the California state appellate courts.

As we drove, we had some sense of what might be troubling John. A profound thinker from the time he was very young, he had always struggled with matters of faith. Going to church and studying for confirmation had never been routine or something to be taken for granted as just a normal part of the life of a pastor's son. Everything was up for grabs, to be questioned, examined, pondered. Nothing was simple for John; everything was made complex and had to be scrutinized from every possible angle.

Many nights when he was in high school and on holiday from college, he would want to stay up late talking about everything including his doubts. "I have a hard time believing in God," he would say, "not because I don't think there may be a God, but it's just that I don't *know*."

Finally when he was in graduate school, he came to the conclusion that he probably was not a Christian. He quit going to church out of a conviction that there was a basic dishonesty in appearing to be what he felt he could not honestly profess to be.

In the past, however, we had never seen him so emotionally upset about his doubts. The agitation that had come to us over the phone was not typical, or so it seemed to us, of a son who had always appeared coolly academic, professional, and articulate.

When we walked into their Santa Monica apartment that night, we were immediately aware that this was to be no ordinary theological discussion with John. Our son appeared to be in crisis, and it soon became apparent to us that this was to be "decision time" for him.

His was a profound crisis of faith and a matter of life and death. The time went quickly as we talked, listened, prayed. When we left, we knew that life had changed for John and Diane.

In the *Los Angeles Times* the next day they saw an ad for an Anglo-Catholic mass in St. Columba's chapel next to the Episcopal Cathedral. They decided to go there. A former Bishop of London once observed that when one first walks into a high-church atmosphere, one is either turned off or intrigued. John was intrigued. During the eucharistic meal (the Lord's Supper or Holy Communion) he sensed the profound "mystery" of Christ in the sacrament.

As John was to say later about this experience, "Perhaps it could be called a 'conversion,' but, if it was that, then it was more evolutionary than revolutionary in nature. Faith, I've learned, is more a matter of conscious decision than of emotion. You have to go beyond your doubts, even if you still have skepticism, and go on into faith."

"Fundamentally," John says, "I still have skepticism, but I have made up my mind to have faith, so then faith exists for me."

Looking back, John perceives the last ten years as years of "daily conversion choices. Like the late great Christian Dorothy Day once said, she never took her faith for granted. It was a gift she received daily, to be held tautly. For her faith was never something she 'possessed.' It was a gift."

Certain events were catalysts leading him to his faith decision. The death of his wife's 55-year-old father that year made John realize that we live in a real world in which we make real decisions with life-and-death consequences. His father-in-law had a history of heart trouble but had made the decision to go back to smoking, drinking coffee, and eating too much in spite of a serious weight problem.

Death, in any shape or form, whether it be the death of someone we love or a confrontation with our own dying, poses questions for believer and unbeliever alike.

"In the academic world," John observes, "there is an embarrassment when it comes to talking about death. The 'secular orthodoxy' among intellectuals prevents us from facing the reality of death as a matter of intelligent inquiry. We can talk about it clinically, but not personally. However, the more I think about it, it seems a bit presumptuous of me to generalize about all intellectuals. I've really known only a small subset, even on my own campus. There may be tremendous variations from discipline to discipline, for all I know."

Like T. S. Eliot, John experienced the "transitoriness and unsatisfactoriness" of life. Although John had often admired celebrated atheists like Mark Twain and Jean-Paul Sartre for their willingness to struggle with cosmic issues to arrive at some sense of the "meaning of life," he began, like Sartre, to have some difficulty with atheism, because you "never get any comfort out of it." The fact that so many unbelievers appeared to be "fighting a good fight of faith" in reverse, struck John as incongruous. As much of their energies were being consumed in doing battle with faith, as believers were expending in the exercise of their faith.

Mark Twain, for instance, had seen his disbelief as a matter of achievement. If you can manage for a whole lifetime not to kid yourself into thinking there's anyone or anything out there, then you've really proved yourself victorious!

At the time of his spiritual crisis John accepted the fact that each one of us must answer our own questions in our own way. We can listen to and read the answers others give, but our answers to the questions of our own life and death must come from our own conscious intent to be personally responsible for the consequences they bring.

John Westerhoff, professor of religion and education at Duke University Divinity School, speaking to a gathering of parish associates told the group that in the development of faith doubt is an essential stage. "Searching faith," he stated, "is the stage in which everything we've heard or learned about God is held out for objective examination."

The doubts expressed during this stage of faith need to be affirmed, and those who hear them do well to take them seriously and be willing to engage in the same struggle toward understanding.

During those high school and college years when John wanted to talk far into the night with anyone who was willing to debate, challenge, or affirm his doubts, we felt that he was wanting to hear how we had worked through the struggles in our faith journey. Later we would hear our responses come back to us in John's own words. If we (inappropriately) asked, "Do you remember when we told you that?" he would not remember. Our responses were not that important to him, but the fact that we were willing to take his struggles seriously was important. Fortunately John married a woman who was also willing to listen to his despairs as he continued his search through graduate school.

All of these conversations and arguments with others are really dialogs within the searcher's own psyche. At the appropriate time, in that moment prepared by the Spirit when all things are ready, all that has been encountered and engaged in the preceding journey becomes the matrix out of which faith becomes a possibility.

That moment, the right time for faith to become one's own, has been called "conversion." We encountered it in the apostle Paul's experience on the Damascus road. We have seen it in John's experience, and we have claimed it as our own experience. Our moments were not as dramatic as Paul's, or as intellectual as John's. They were our own.

To the degree that our past journey was one of skepticism and doubt, we will probably recall our conversion as a time of great enlightenment, a time of complete change of perspective and direction.

As an expression of the fact that this particular "faith" that they now own is uniquely theirs, new "converts" may reject some of their previous affiliations out of a conscious need to assert their ownership of that faith.

John and Diane chose to join another denomination than the ones in which they had grown up. Such a decision should not be perceived by others as a rejection of them, but simply as an affirmation of the convert's own commitments.

John's choice of a church with which to affiliate had to be compatible with his own identity and needs. Always interested in history, needing structure in his life, John was drawn to the Episcopal Church. The Eucharist became the event through which the risen Christ became immanent in his life. The Anglican conviction of continuity with the ancient church appealed to him. The order and structure of the worship service comforts and sustains him.

As John says, "You have to answer the questions in your own way, and those questions go beyond denominational preferences. There are substratum questions of far more importance. I knew that I had to have a fellowship that allowed for intellectual inquiry and that respected history and tradition, both of which are my own values."

John will always be a skeptic, but now he's a believing skeptic.

The Gospels record the story of a man whose reply of believing skepticism has become a classic response. In an early description of the event Mark recounted how Jesus and three of his disciples—Peter, James, and John—had gone up on a mountaintop, high enough so that clouds surrounded them. There they experienced what we call the Transfiguration, when Jesus assumed the transparent glory he knew before his coming to earth, and two Old Testament personages, Moses and Elijah, appeared with him (Mark 9:2-13).

The faith of the disciples was affirmed, and they knew beyond a doubt who Jesus was. Of course, the three of them wanted to stay up there on the mountain in an atmosphere that made faith easy.

But to go down from the mountain is imperative.

There, at the foot of the mountain, was being enacted just the kind of scenario in which skepticism flourishes. The other disciples were arguing with the scribes, those ancient interpreters of the law (Mark 9:14-32).

The first question Jesus asked his disciples was, "What are you arguing with them about?"

The problem they faced was one that could not be solved with discussions or interpretations of biblical texts. The problem was one of faith, and, according to Jesus, that was a matter of prayer. Faith was needed to heal the man's epileptic son, but, lacking faith, the disciples "could not."

The father who had asked the disciples to do the healing did not really believe that Jesus could do anything about his son either, because he said, skeptically, "*If* you can do anything, take pity on us and help us." Skepticism always tests, examines, probes. It doubts that love is unconditional, nonjudgmental, seeking the best for everyone.

Jesus did not reject the doubter but responded to the father's doubts as an honest expression of "searching faith." "'If you can'?" he said. "Everything is possible for him who believes."

The father's answer, true to his character, is the ongoing response of the skeptic. "I do believe; help me overcome my unbelief!"

Don't be afraid of your doubts. Jesus can stand any test to which he can be put. If he can't, then he is not worthy to be your Lord. In fact, one might begin to believe from the evidence that Jesus welcomes testing. Questioning gives him an opportunity to provide additional evidence for our assurance.

One of his disciples has earned the nickname of "Doubting Thomas," because he wanted firsthand evidence that Jesus had truly risen from the dead (John 20:19-29). When the other disciples told him that they had *seen* the risen Jesus, that he had come to them in the locked upper room where they were hiding for fear that they might suffer the same fate Jesus had suffered, Thomas scoffed in disbelief. "Look," he said, "how do I know it was Jesus you saw? I want proof! Unless I see in his hands the print of the nails, and place my finger in the mark of the nails, and place my hand in his side where he was wounded, I will not believe!"

A week later when the disciples were again together and Thomas was with them, Jesus responded to Thomas's skepticism with an invitation. "Here," he said, holding out his nail-scarred hands, "put your finger here. What are you waiting for, Thomas? Look at my hands! And, here, put out your hand and place it in my wounded side. Just don't be faithless, but believe."

We don't know if Thomas responded with a touch of his hand, but he was convinced and answered Jesus, "My Lord and my God!"

Jesus then said to him, "Because you have seen me, you have believed; blessed are those who have not seen and yet have believed."

But if Thomas had not challenged Jesus with his skepticism, we would have been denied this convincing testimony to the physical reality of Jesus' resurrected body. The expressed doubts of Thomas have provided us with corroborating evidence that the postresurrection body of Jesus still bore the marks of his crucifixion, marks he will bear throughout eternity on our behalf.

The one thing Jesus cannot stand is apathy, the uncaring ho hum of lukewarm disinterest. "Would that you were cold or hot!" he said to the church in Laodicea. "So, because you are lukewarm—neither hot nor cold—I am about to spit you out of my mouth" (Rev. 3:16).

Doubts must sometimes be seen, however, as a temptation from the devil to deny Jesus and to steal away the Christian's joy and assurance. Then they must be dealt with very promptly and as the evil they are.

Jim, who had been a pastor in another Protestant church for more than 50 years, called me one Sunday afternoon. His voice held the same note of desperation that had been in John's voice that midnight hour of his despair. "Sister Marge," he said, "could I see you this afternoon? I must talk to you! I'm in great desperation!"

Jim knew us through reading our books. We had written about Erling's recovery from his broken neck and paralysis, and Jim had been given our books a couple of years after that as a Christmas present. When we met him, he told us that he kept the books on his bedside table and would read them before he went to bed, as a reminder of the healing presence of Jesus. In fact, when he brought his copies to us for autographing, we noticed how worn they were and how thoroughly they had been underlined and marked.

Because I had a full schedule of engagements for the rest of the day, I responded with some regret to his request for an appointment that Sunday afternoon. "But I can meet you here at the church at ten o'clock tomorrow morning," I said. "Can you be here then?"

"I'll be there," he said. "I'll make myself hang on until then."

Jim was waiting for me when I pulled into the parking

lot the next morning. When he greeted me, his face was working with emotion and he was fighting back tears.

I drew him quickly into a vacant office, and he broke down as he sobbed out his story.

"Oh, Sister Marge," he said, struggling for control, "I've been a minister for all these years and I've brought hundreds of people to the Lord and helped many of them through their dying moments. But now that I'm over 80 and near my own time of death, I'm not sure that what I've been preaching all these years is really true!" More sobbing. I waited, and Jim went on. "I keep asking myself, 'What if it's all a lie? What if it never happened and Jesus was just a man and the resurrection was a fraud?' It's driving me crazy. I can't eat, my sleep is disturbed, and I'm afraid that I'm committing a sin just by thinking these things!"

Which one of us has never thought such thoughts or asked such questions?

"I believe, Lord; help me overcome my unbelief!" That theme plays counterpoint to our faith.

I knew that Brother Jim believed. All he needed at that moment was to be accepted even in his unbelief and to be led ever so gently and firmly back to the reality of his faith. To scold, or belittle his doubts, or try to laugh them away would not help. My heart ached for the pain that was so evident in his body.

"Brother Jim," I started, not really sure what I could say. "Brother Jim, I love you, and I know God loves you, too." At that moment that fact was one thing I was sure of. "Brother Jim, have you been baptized?" He looked up, startled by the abruptness of my question. "Yes, yes, of course, I'm baptized. I made my decision for Jesus when I was six years old."

"Did you believe then that Jesus died on the cross for you?"

"Oh, yes, I really did. And I knew then that I would give my life to follow him and to serve him!"

"Have you ever taken back your commitment to follow him?"

"No, if I had it to do all over again, I'd live my life the same way."

"Then you have nothing to worry about, do you?" I asked him. "In the Gospel according to Mark we are told that the one who believes and is baptized shall be saved. Do you believe that?"

Again, without hesitation, he said, "I do believe that, and I've told that to many other people. Yes, of course," his eyes were dry now and the sparkle was returning to them. His chin had stopped its trembling.

Then he jumped up as though he had received a massive dose of energy.

"I know it, I *know* it!" he shouted. "Oh, Sister Marge, I feel like my life has been renewed. I'm going to go home and get started on that book I've always wanted to write! It's going to have 12 chapters just like the 12 apostles. I'm going to get started right away!"

We hugged each other, we prayed and he left.

I watched him through the office window as he went to his car, almost running and doing a little skipping step now and then.

His doubts had forced him to turn for help. He let them work for him instead of against him. When I last heard of Jim he was getting along fine. His tired body was wearing out and giving him some problems but his spirit was released and joyous.

"Faith is not an emotion," said John, "but a conscious decision. Fundamentally, I have skepticism, but I go beyond that and have faith."

Unless we can get beyond our unbelief, we will never experience the fact of God's love.

The hardest thing in the world to believe is that God loves *me*.

"Lord, help my unbelief!" must be the cry that moves us beyond skepticism to faith. The decision is ours.

And love is there waiting.

Nine

THE BELOVED COMMUNITY

Monday morning, ten o'clock. At the university where I teach, a church-related college in California, it was "forum" time. Four hundred students, mostly freshmen completing this final phase of their Freshman Colloquium, and some of their faculty, had gathered in the gym-auditorium to listen to five of their fellow students, three women and two men, give their responses to all of the visiting "experts" who had spoken to them in preceding weeks.

Four of the five had already given their speeches. The audience applauded each of them very vigorously with whistles and shouts, visibly impressed by their articulate and well-thought-out summaries of the series.

Then the fifth student, Shawn, came to the microphone. Much shorter than the other presenters, she pulled the mike down to her level. If she was nervous, it did not show.

But the others were a hard act to follow. They had vividly and thoroughly rehearsed all that the forum lecturers had said about the university's theme for the year, "Extended Families; Shared Lives." A black South African had impressed them with his graphic descriptions of the horrors of apartheid for his people. A professor from El Salvador had given a moving history of his homeland, climaxing it with an emotional description of the struggle going on in the present. Additional speakers had included a woman, the child of an alcoholic, who had given an honest portrayal of the effects of alcoholic parents on the life of the family. A career counselor, a lawyer, a business leader, an expert on the changing roles of men and women—all had confronted the students with their ideas and challenges.

The four students appeared to have impressed the audience even more than had the experts to whom they were reacting. Now it was Shawn's turn. How could she embellish what had already been said? She started by admitting that there was not much that had been left unsaid about the forum series. "So," she said, "instead of reacting to the speakers who have presented the theme for the year, I'm going to speak on the theme itself."

She began by talking about her journey from her home in Minnesota to attend college in California. "I love my family," she went on, "and I knew when I decided to come to California for college that it would probably be hard for both them and for me to be so far away from each other. We've always been very close. But I knew that I had to grow up and go away from home some day. Other people had survived leaving their families and being separated by many miles, so I thought I would survive, too."

For a while it was exciting to be away and on her own, she told the audience, but then she began to miss her family more and more. Birthdays, holidays, family outings—she was missing them all.

"Other students were having the same feelings," she

said, "so we would get together and comfort one another. We were all experiencing some homesickness. I wondered how the students who were here from other countries, some still trying to learn English, separated from their families by oceans, how they could stand it."

November came. That's when Shawn's nagging homesickness became acute. She could not afford to go home at Thanksgiving and Christmas, too. The logical thing to do was to stay at school until Christmas and then go home.

One by one, the other students shared their plans for Thanksgiving. Talk of home cooking, brothers and sisters, the kids at the home church, and high school friends was everywhere. The week of Thanksgiving came, and no one seemed to want to study or to go to classes any more. Emotionally, the students had already packed their suitcases and hopped on their planes to go *home*. Shawn was ready to say good-bye to everyone else in the dorm and prepared herself for a totally lonely Thanksgiving holiday.

"That's when I learned," her speech went on, "what the theme for this year really means. I experienced what it means to have an extended family and shared lives. I hadn't been too successful in identifying with the people in South Africa or El Salvador, even though I do care about their problems and wish I could do more to help them. But the world, the whole world, as my extended family just wasn't real to me."

Then she described the moment when the theme became real and personal for her. "I couldn't believe it," she said, her eyes lighting up, "when a couple of my friends came to my room and handed me an envelope. I opened it, and a plane ticket fell out. 'I don't understand,' I said, 'what's this for?' When they told me that 25 of my friends had gotten together and contributed enough money to buy me a round-trip plane ticket so I could go home for Thanksgiving, I just couldn't believe it! Even some kids I didn't know had given money so that I could be with my family."

The audience, sitting on the uncomfortable bleachers or on squeaky steel folding chairs on the basketball court, was very, very quiet. Only the noise of a passing motorcycle broke the silence.

Shawn continued. "Now I know what the theme is all about. It's caring about the pain of every other human being in our world. We all need each other. Every one of us on this earth is related in some way. If not through family, or race, or national citizenship, then we're related because we are all children of God who loves us and loves every other person through us."

Our speaker sat down. The series had come together. We all knew in a personal way what the year's theme was all about.

The church is our ultimate "family," the visible sign of Christ's presence in the world. The word used for *church* in the New Testament is a Greek word *ecclesia,* which means "called out." The church is simply those persons called out by Jesus to follow him.

Although *ecclesia* is found many times in the New Testament, it occurs only three times in the Gospels, and all three of those occurrences are in the Gospel according to Matthew.

Jesus is reported by Matthew to have used it the first time on the occasion of Peter's confession, "You are the Christ, the Son of the living God" (Matt. 16:16). In response Jesus said that he would build his "church" on that God-given insight and confession of Peter (16:18).

The next two times the word *ecclesia* is used in Matthew are in Chapter 18, where Jesus tells his disciples how to deal with offenders in the church, a procedure we know as "church discipline" (18:17).

Although Jesus did not talk much about the church, he spent his time here on earth demonstrating the nature of the *ecclesia*, that beloved called-out community of his.

He called some people to follow him and they became his disciples, both men and women (Luke 8:1-3). He taught them all about the kingdom he had come to establish, describing it in parables (stories) and giving them signs of its presence through healings, natural wonders, and raising the dead.

Wherever he went, through cities and villages, in mountain areas and desert wildernesses, his little community of disciples went with him. They slept together, ate together, were human together. He understood their humanity, their weaknesses and their doubts. They heard him pray in intimate terms to the One whom he addressed as "Abba-Daddy."

Jesus knew that when he was no longer with them, when he had fulfilled his "mission," had suffered the death he had come to die and accomplished the resurrection which he had promised to give them, then the little community would be scattered (Matt. 26:31).

But that small group of followers was essential to the future of the kingdom of God. Without them, all that God had sacrificed through the death of Jesus, all the love that had been poured out for the life of the world, would be lost to the memory of humankind. The community had to live!

Yet how could that scattered, fearful group of illiterate, common men and women, ex-fishermen, ex-tax-collector, ex-demon-possessed, ex-all those things that all of us are—how could these few, this little community, become the presence of Christ in the whole world, proclaiming the good news that the kingdom of God had come?

In his final appearance to this powerless band of human beings, Jesus gave them the promise of transforming power. They were to wait right there in Jerusalem, and he would send his Holy Spirit to them. That Spirit would give them power to be his witnesses not only right there in the very center of the people of God, but also in the neighboring villages and provinces and right on out to the very "ends of the earth" (Acts 1:8).

This little group of fearful humans? Any interested observer of the disciples would have said it was impossible.

Ever since Jesus' crucifixion, 43 days before this, the whole group had really never been in the same place at the same time. Judas, one of the 12 apostles, had betrayed Jesus and had killed himself (Matt. 27:3-5). Peter had denied Jesus and gone back to Galilee to fish with Thomas, Nathanael, James and John, and two others (John 21:1-3).

About 120 persons were left in the little community of followers. On the day of the Jewish harvest festival of Pentecost, just 10 days after they had seen Jesus for the last time and had received his promise of the Spirit's coming, they were—miracle of miracles!—together in one place. Being together in one place is a significant descriptor for the beginning of "the beloved community." Signs and wonders are possible when the people of God get together with one accord and devote themselves to prayer!

The little band of Jesus' friends did just that (Acts 1:14). Jesus himself had told them that this is exactly the kind of environment in which he himself is present (Matt. 18:19-20).

Out of that time of togetherness, in the midst of their gathering, the Holy Spirit came with power, according to the promise. All of the accompanying phenomena, the rushing wind and tongues of fire, testified to the new Spirit that would forge a new people with a new message and send them out into the world to proclaim, "Repent, for the kingdom of God is at hand!"

The church, the beloved community, was born. The called-out ones, coming together in their small gatherings, were the new body of Christ in the world, completing in and through its fellowship the work of the Christ.

Because he saw the survival of the gospel to be dependent on communities of believers, serving one another and accountable to each other, the apostle Paul spent his life gathering people together in small groups in the cities of his world—in places like Ephesus, Philippi, Corinth, Thessalonica, until he had organized the followers of Jesus into congregations that dotted the entire Roman Empire in one generation. Of course, he did not do this single-handedly. There were others, some of their names known to us, others totally unknown, who shouted and whispered the name of Jesus everywhere they went.

And everywhere those who knew that name began to gather in house churches, by the riverside, in caves, in graveyards, in servant's quarters, in Roman guardhouses, to share the teachings of Jesus, to pray, to share the wine and bread of the Lord's Supper, and to help the poor among them.

Gathered in the name of Jesus, they were part of a worldwide—and, according to Paul, even a cosmic—body whose directing head was their Lord Jesus Christ. In the letter to the Ephesians, with great sweeping strokes, Paul painted his pictures of this great body of believers to show how Jesus becomes visible and available.

Through his church Jesus straddles two worlds. Those who are associated with him inhabit two "countries," with their citizenship in heaven as well as on earth.

Their rights to the world to come are already purchased by the cross and resurrection of Jesus. For that reason they already belong to a kingdom that is both here and yet to come. This divine certainty ought to make them the envy of all those who see their assurance. Both time and eternity are their possession. They have it *all* now!

Inside those two worlds, the music of worship ebbs and flows around Jesus and his body, the church, the living temple of God. Peter and Paul both saw this temple, built of "living" stones, as a center of worship, luminous and transparent, through which all of the world can see the glory of God.

The Spirit struggles with Christians to help them grow into receivers and transparencies of the glory of God. When the church surrenders to the Spirit, it becomes an irresistible magnet drawing people—all people—into its fellowship. Being with them is to experience the presence of God.

Unfortunately, some people never get close enough to a church to experience that sense of community. They are suspicious of "organized" groups, they tell us. They call attention to the history of wars fought in the name of God and supported by the church. They remember every story they've ever heard in which the leadership of the church has oppressed people, swindled them, and conducted inquisitions and witch hunts. They recall every schism and conflict that's split the church.

So they know nothing about the hundreds of faithful and sharing church fellowships that keep love alive in our world. They never encounter the communities of loving people meeting on every continent of our globe, welcoming the stranger, providing sanctuary for the homeless and the hopeless, contributing to the vast outpouring of charitable and mission support that keeps our world a humane place in which to live.

Try to imagine, if you will, the immense and ubiquitous network of gatherings in their individual parts. We have met with them in mud patios in Mexico, where "base communities" of poor people gather around the Bible, teaching each other to read the words, and sharing in their "love feasts."

In Taipei we gathered with students in a church near the university, and, although we knew no words of Chinese, we understood what the worshipers were saying and singing.

Behind the Iron Curtain, near Budapest, the ancient and beautiful city on the Danube, we worshiped with a congregation in the rural village of Csömör. Tears choked us as these Christians sang the ancient hymns so heartily that the flowers on the altar trembled!

In every conceivable setting, with people of all races and under diverse political regimes, Christians continue to gather, called together by the ringing of bells from the steeples of city cathedrals and white rural churches, by the beat of African drums, by whispered invitations and newspaper advertisements, and by the cry in their own hearts.

They come together—the rich in their limousines, the poor on foot. The lame, the halt, and the blind are among them, the strong and the weak, the solemn and the joyful, the young and the old, gathering to experience the "communion of saints."

For almost 2000 years they've come by the millions, drowned to their old life in the waters of Baptism, rising with Christ to newness of life in the church of Jesus, sinners made saints in the name of Jesus Christ.

For all these years an unbroken proclamation of God's Word and an unbroken celebration of the Holy Communion has kept the *ecclesia* faithful to its mission in the world. The words "This is my body broken for you," repeated in many tongues, in many lands, under many conditions, ever since Christians first began to gather—those words have sustained, fed, and nourished the church through the ages.

Shawn had experienced in a very personal way exactly what the true nature of the church is.

In its ideal sense the church is still that fellowship of which it can be said that "all the believers were one in heart and mind. No one claimed that any of his possessions was his own, but they shared everything they had" (Acts 4:32).

It was out of that context that the apostles with great power "continued to testify to the resurrection of the Lord Jesus, and much grace was upon them all" (4:33). Being of one heart and mind and having everything in common inevitably leads to great power for witness and great grace for the community.

Because of the gift that her community had given to Shawn, great grace came upon all of us gathered in the gym on that final forum day of the year. For one fleeting Camelot moment, the love of God turned our old Butler-building gymnasium into a cathedral bathed with love. The church, the beloved community, God's extended family, had been recreated for Shawn and all of us by a plane ticket, caring friends, and a young woman who was able to go home for Thanksgiving.

Ten

LOVE'S CONNECTION

Prayer keeps one connected to the love of God. Therefore, "unceasing prayer" is the Christian's goal. At one time in my (Erling's) life, unceasing prayer "happened" for me.

In the opening chapter of this book I talked about being prepared by my childhood relationship with my father for a life committed to hard work. The daily discipline of prayer became part of that "work," never to be neglected.

I was caught up by the intensity of the prayers of Jesus. His heart burned with the desire to be in constant communication with God. The intimacy of his prayer life was the environment in which he chose to live. I was fascinated by his frequent withdrawal into the desert to pray alone. His ability to pray through the night and still be fresh enough to continue his ministry in the morning was an unmet challenge to me.

I marveled at the total confidence with which he stood at the grave of Lazarus and thanked God for always hearing his petitions. The final march to his death was undergirded by his anguished prayer in the garden of Gethsemane where he poured out his pain and purpose to God and won the struggle with his fear. His resolve to complete God's will in his life rebuked my often vacillating heart.

I hungered for his kind of relationship with God. I wanted more than anything else to have this kind of experience of intimate prayer for myself.

Then it happened to me in a way I would never have sought. I was body surfing at Laguna Beach on the south coast of California one August afternoon, when an unexpected wave picked me up and smashed me against the ocean floor. My neck was broken, three fractured vertebrae crushed my spinal cord, and I was totally paralyzed from the neck down. I could not move at all. I had to be fed, shaved, bathed. I was helpless.

Life had forced me into my own "place apart." In the desert of my experience I learned to pray all night. In my spirit I roamed freely across the landscape of my memory. Time and space were no longer a problem for me in my paralysis. I visited places and people throughout the night, sensing their needs, presenting those needs to God, bathing them with prayer. I found my own spirit fed as I lifted others into the presence of God.

New dimensions of God's love revealed themselves to me. I prayed all night and barely touched the throngs who needed God to hear their cries for love. The Spirit brought them to my mind, all of the people I had not really thought about in any intentional way for many years.

They were in my hospital room with me, representatives of the vast ocean of need on our globe, but I knew that the hundreds I could envision and pray for were just a small part of, just an infinitesimal drop in that global ocean of pain.

"Wide, wide as the ocean, deep, deep as the sea"—the words of a gospel hymn described so well the immensity of

God's ocean of love. "High, high as the heavens above"—
and my spirit soared in my paralyzed body with the words
that sang in my mind.

No wonder the New Testament had to find a word for
the gracious, unmerited, unconditional love of God—*agape*.
What a marvelous word, never found as a word for love
anywhere else in classical Greek writings, a uniquely Christian word for the love of God. Different from friendship,
from the love between a man and woman, from the love of
parent and child, *agape* describes only the unmerited, un-
reserved, freely given love of God.

Plato, the philosopher, had written a great deal about
eros, the love that he said could bring humans into the very
presence of God. *Eros* was a love that one worked to achieve.
By diligent effort one could attain that kind of love for God.

The New Testament, on the other hand, describes
agape as the love of God that one does not have to work to
achieve. It is freely given, available to anyone who wants it
through the Christ in whom it was personified and dem-
onstrated. Because it demands nothing from the one who
receives its gift, *agape* ignites a responding love in the heart
of the receiver.

Prayer, then, is not only our connection to the love of
God, but it is the channel through which *agape* is made
available to all whose cry is, "For God's sake, love me!"

I learned the necessity of being free from all distractions
if one is to experience prayer as a complete dedication to a
task—the task of making a love connection, of being a love
channel, between God and the Creator's world.

Although my "place apart" had been forced on me, I
was to realize it as a mark of God's love, giving me what
my spirit had longed for, a lesson in Christ-like prayer.

Don't ask me what I might have felt and thought if the
doctor's prediction that I would never walk to work again

had come true and my enforced inactivity had lasted the rest of my life! I really don't know.

All I knew was that at the time I was praying all night in the hospital, I was immensely grateful for the privilege of a time, as well as a place, apart.

Ever since my recovery and return to work, the struggle has been to try to maintain my ardor and zeal for that complete focus on prayer.

It wasn't that I came out of the hospital with the conviction that prayer was okay while I was paralyzed because it was the only thing I could do at that time and now it was time to get on with the real work again. Not at all. I *knew* that my prayers had made a difference in the lives of the people I prayed for. Perhaps my prayers had accomplished more real work than any I had ever done when I was physically energetic. Who can say?

Things happened as a result of prayer. One night I was moved to focus prayer concern on another pastor whom I had not seen for some years, and I am certain that I had never prayed for him before in my life. Early that morning the telephone at my bedside rang, and when the nurse had placed the phone next to my ear, I was startled to hear the voice of the very pastor I had been praying for that night! He was calling to ask for prayers for a physical condition he had just been made aware of, and I had come to his mind.

Another time after my prayer had been concerned with a patient whom I had met in treatment in the hospital, she came into my room to tell me that she was leaving the hospital. The doctor could find no trace of the cancer from which she was supposed to be dying.

Prayer, I had learned, was as important and meaningful a work as any I had ever done in my physically active days.

After a year of rehabilitation following the accident, I came back to my congregation and to active parish ministry.

Immediately I was immersed in the congregation's agenda. Of course, I loved every minute of it, but my prayer life soon returned to its usual habit, the routine of morning and evening prayer, grace at the table, and, when we could get the family together, family prayers.

Marge was in another city working at the job she had gone to in order to support our family during my convalescence. I had no partner in prayer to serve as a spiritual mentor to me. Nor did she, in her tremendously taxing position, find anyone who could relate to her in that way. We were on our own, lonely islands in a sea of distractions in both of our lives.

Is that the story of your life? Some of you still have children at home. Others are struggling to finish graduate school or to succeed in a new career. We understand the difficulty of finding any time or place apart when all of these things demand so much time and energy. And in most busy households where children and extended family members live there is no place apart to be found.

When our children were at home, we felt we were each doing well to snatch our own moments alone to pray. Trying to find time to pray together only led to constant frustration. With five children in various stages of need, each with his or her own pattern of sleep, we found little waking time for joining together in prayer. Family devotional times did not serve the purposes of a rich prayer life, and by the time we had prayed with each of the children at their individual bedtimes, we often were too tired to pray together.

Of course we managed to keep our prayer lists and to remember those for whom we had pledged to pray, but the need to withdraw to a place apart remained an acute unmet need in our lives.

Obviously it was that same need that drove, and still

drives, people into monastic communities, where they can explore the silent reaches of their souls.

Is all lost as far as prayer is concerned if one cannot pray in whatever way one considers the *ideal* way to pray? or which someone else informs us is the ideal way to pray? Not at all. Even though one's prayer is no more than an upward glance throughout the day, a one-word cry for help, a word of praise, the glad thought of God in the morning, or the last vision of God before falling asleep, it is the habit of prayer that operates like a flywheel to keep one's life of prayer from falling into total disrepair.

When we acknowledge that prayer is not just *our* work, but a means provided by the *agape* of God whereby God keeps in touch with us, the whole matter is seen in proper perspective. "Prayer is to religion what original research is to science," said P. T. Forsythe.

We keep on searching, looking for new ways to keep the prayer connection vital and pulsing with fresh life. We test and explore new avenues through which to move into deeper, more significant areas and levels of prayer.

Basic to the development of unceasing prayer is an understanding of the value of meditation. Meditation can take place anywhere, on a plane, in the office, in a kitchen, anywhere. Meditation permits the mind to be absorbed in some reality outside of oneself. For instance, one can become absorbed in the warmth and wonder of a single word or phrase in a worship service or become lost in the beauty of a flower or a sunset that tantalizes the spirit with the creative glory of God.

A rosebush or a bird feeder outside a window can become the object of meditation.

Absorb a phrase, a verse, a story, some segment of the Bible and spend a day, a week, a month draining it, through many an odd moment of meditation, of all of its meaning until it catches fire in your spirit.

Meditation remains a basic aspect of prayer, because it feeds the spirit by expanding meaning, exercising the imagination, and coloring devotional feelings. It provides assurance of the presence of God, strengthens our sense of security, and gives new visions of the glory of Christ.

Meditation is not emptying oneself, but absorbing into one's spirit the endless facets of God's presence and all of the profound treasures of the Scripture. Everything the senses have transmitted to the mind becomes the stuff on which meditation feeds. The apostle Paul said that what God has given us is immeasurably more than all that we can ask or imagine (Eph. 3:20).

As helpful as meditation is, we have found that the practice of contemplative prayer goes beyond meditation and enriches all of prayer for us. Contemplative prayer provides a profound possibility, a releasing for ministry, which meditation cannot give. Because meditation absorbs the objects of meditation, it may become closed in on itself. One may never risk gambling one's life for God. The mystery of the love of Jesus demands that we lose ourselves, abandon our life, in him.

Contemplative prayer seeks Jesus *for his own sake.* Unlike meditation, it asks for nothing and does not go outside of itself to find an object to contemplate. Contemplation seeks only for the emptiness which is kept for God, clear of everything and anything else.

Early Christians lost themselves in repeating the name of Jesus, minutes on end. They reveled in the privilege of being in his presence, loving him for his own sake. Their prayers were often simple ones, like "Jesus, Son of God, have mercy on me." For them the *name* of Jesus was therapeutic.

Healing came to a man lame from birth when Peter told him to walk "in the name of Jesus Christ of Nazareth." When questioned about the event, Peter told the people that the man was made strong by Jesus' name, by faith in his name (Acts 3).

When the leaders of the Temple understood the power in the name of Jesus, they conferred with one another and decided to warn them to "speak no longer to anyone in this name." Then they called them and charged them not to speak or teach at all in the name of Jesus (Acts 4:17-18).

The name brings the person.

One of the profound differences between the Old and New Testaments lies in attitudes toward the use of the name of God. The Old Testament worshipers hesitated to speak or write the name of God, considering it too holy to be mentioned. In the Dead Sea Scrolls, the manuscripts of the Old Testament Scriptures discovered in 1947 near the Dead Sea, the name of Yahweh is indicated by four dots ". . . ." that stand for the Hebrew letters YHWH. But in the New Testament, power comes with the frequent use of the name of Jesus. In Paul's letter to the Philippians the name of God in a variety of combinations appears 71 times in the 104 verses of the letter.

And it's the simple name of Jesus, in the only instance in which it appears alone and not in combination with one of his other names, that has the most power of all. Paul tells us it's that simple name, the name of Jesus itself, which will cause every knee to bow, "in heaven and on earth and under the earth, and every tongue confess that Jesus Christ is Lord, to the glory of God the Father" (Phil. 2:10-11).

So it's the name of Jesus, alone or in any combination of his names, that evokes all of the grace that the incarnate God came to provide. Since God is love, every prayerful repetition of that name bonds one more tightly to God in love.

When, through focusing on the name and person of Jesus, we begin to catch even a glimpse of the glory that is his, we hunger for more. The pent-up, burning desire of our own hearts echoes Paul's cry, "That I may know him and the power of his resurrection!" Our psyche longs to penetrate all the facades that block us from God's presence. We thirst for an existential, mystical encounter with the reality of God's presence, to know the depths and riches of Christ Jesus our Lord. We find ourselves living in prayerful expectancy, straining to stand on spiritual tiptoe, wanting no competitor to Jesus in our lives.

Contemplative prayer permits us to engage in the struggle to become intimately involved with Jesus. We are abandoned to, and absorbed in, the being of Jesus. Only in the naked vulnerability of the contemplative state can we discover who he is and who we are in our inmost persons as children of God.

Although contemplative prayer is not complex, it is not to be entered into lightly. When one settles down into this kind of intensity of prayer and begins to see all of life through the eyes of Jesus, you discover that you are no longer your own but you are under the lordship of Jesus. You have let yourself be freed from all of the distractions that have saturated your life before.

Contemplative prayer calls for two disciplines.

The first of these makes it possible to have a life of unceasing prayer even in the midst of a busy schedule. Select a simple prayer no longer than a "breath," about six to eight words long. Let that prayer come out of your particular place of "brokenness," the place in you that needs the touch of Jesus. Your need may be for peace. Your breath prayer could be the simple cry, "Jesus, child of God, give me peace!" Or your need may be for patience. In that case a breath prayer could be, "Jesus, Son of God, give me patience."

Search your spirit for the place in you that needs healing, and in your prayer, invoke the name of Jesus and one of his attributes, and add your petition. How easy it becomes to say this brief but significant prayer a dozen or more times a day! So many minutes are wasted between our activities that can become significant moments of contemplation as our thoughts are directed, in the name of Jesus, to the person of Jesus.

The second discipline is that of "a place apart." Just five, ten, fifteen minutes is enough to begin the practice. Set a timer (preferably one that does not make a ticking sound), close your eyes, and focus on your brief prayer until the timer calls you back from your retreat into prayer. At first it will take all of your ability to concentrate, to stay with your sentence prayer for even five minutes.

Have a notebook handy, and when your time is up, write down any thoughts that you need to express. The goal is not to experience any phenomena, such as visions, sounds, words, or messages, but to empty that place in us that is reserved for God, to clean it out of all the distractions that have cluttered it and kept us from seeing Jesus.

Your experience of being closeted with Jesus himself will grow, and eventually you will be able to focus on his person for a much longer period of time.

All of the New Testament witnesses affirm the enormity of Jesus. They see in him the creator of everything and everyone, the Savior of the whole world, and the final judge of every human being. The more we dare to follow this Savior, the greater he becomes. The more we let ourselves be caught up by him, the deeper our discovery of the miracle given us by his Spirit that "if anyone is in Christ, he is a new creation; the old has gone, the new has come" (2 Cor. 5:17).

A new creation! Imagine being carried back in time to the primal moments of the first creation, sensing that self-same Spirit brooding over the face of the deep. In those first moments of cosmic formlessness the Spirit began the vast creativity that formed the universe, all of its massiveness and glory. With ease, the Spirit spun off galaxies of stars and, at the same time, formed the intricate delicacy of a flower or a snowflake.

More than all, the Spirit designed humans to be formed in the inner likeness of God. This, the Scripture affirms, can happen to you again and again. You can be a new creation where change and renewal is a constant gift.

On the one hand, your life-style can be drastically simplified, your rabid, frantic racing after a name or fame or things wiped away. If we dare live Paul's simple statement of purpose: "One thing I do: Forgetting what is behind and straining toward what is ahead, I press on toward the goal to win the prize for which God has called me heavenward in Christ Jesus," we breathe in freedom again (Phil. 3:13-14).

On the other hand, you find yourself able to transform even the ugliest dimensions of your life into ultimate victories.

Vividly alive in our memory is the picture of the black pastoral activist living in South Africa, Simon Farisani. In an address to the 7th Assembly of the Lutheran World Federation in Budapest in 1984, he told the gathering how he had been beaten mercilessly and then shocked by massive doses of electricity when the white police arrested and tortured him for speaking out against apartheid. Because he lives with the reality of his Lord, Jesus Christ, he was able to tell them, even in the face of their laughter and mockery, that he loved them and was praying for them.

Through prayer we are connected with the God who is love.

Prayer makes us vulnerable to the demands of love by absorbing us into noble and selfless grandeur. The Spirit enables us to live out again the life of Jesus, to build him up in people, to make him great. We carry God around in us, fulfilling our ministries.

We have come full circle in our emptiness and lonely cry for love.

Through our "love connection" the God-shaped emptiness in us becomes the cradle filled with Jesus and we become, with him, God's word made flesh.

Marked with the sign of the cross in our baptism, we live out God's cruciform life of love in our needy world.

In Christ, we who share his life become God's answer to the echoing cry, "For God's sake, love me!"